STEAMING INTO THE NORTH WEST

Tales of the Premier Line

Michael Clutterbuck

HEDDON PUBLISHING

www.heddonpublishing.com
www.facebook.com/heddonpublishing
@PublishHeddon

This book is for Ian Norman, friend (and LNWR Mentor) of many years who showed me that the Great Western was not the only railway worthy of study.

Introduction

To my very great regret, Ian Norman, to whom this book is dedicated, passed away shortly after publication. Ian was an inspirational modeller and a close friend, who is deeply missed by his family and his many friends and admirers here in Australia as well as in the UK.

Since the first edition was published, a number of readers have expressed disappointment at the brevity of the book, so I decided to lengthen it to bring it into line with the others of the *Steaming Into* series. I have gone back to the original constituent companies which formed the LNWR in 1846 for the first stories.

The London and North Western Railway, like most of the private railways in the UK before 1923, had its heyday in the first decade of the 20th century. At the time, the LNWR was possibly the world's largest private company and was known in the UK as 'The Premier Line'. It was formed by a merger of the London and Birmingham Railway and the Grand Junction Railway in 1846; its headquarters were at Euston and its locomotive works were at Crewe. By 1900 the company was even producing its own steel in Crewe Works.

Although my own main interest is in the Great Western Railway, I got to know something of the LNWR when I met Ian Norman in Melbourne over 20 years ago; his Gauge O model of LNWR practice is inspirational (and has provided the cover photo). Through him, I have come to appreciate some of the qualities which made the LNWR so successful. This series of short stories is intended to provide a brief glimpse of life on the London and North Western Railway in the years immediately before the First World War.

I have long been disappointed in the dearth of railway fiction compared with crime or war stories and decided to write some, if only to entertain myself. The fact that my efforts have reached publication has been a constant surprise and I am extremely grateful for the expert work of Katharine Smith of Heddon Publishing, who is largely responsible for the success of the *Steaming Into* series. I am also indebted to the meticulous checking of technical detail by Dr John Ritter of Melbourne, and have also been fortunate to be able to include an episode based on the personal experience of Mr Ron Stockton, himself once a fireman with the LMS.

Mike Clutterbuck,
Melbourne 2017

Main lines referred to in the stories

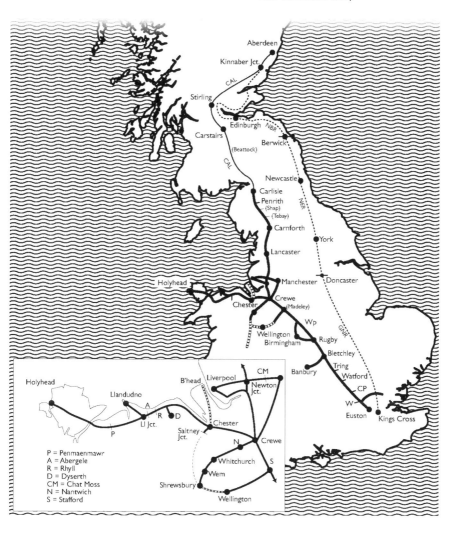

LNWR
LNWR & GWR join
Caledonian Railway
Other railways

CP = Carpenders Park
Ll J = Llandudno Junction
Wp = Wolverhampton
W = Willesden
( ) = Steep banks
NER = North Eastern Railway

P = Penmaenmawr
A = Abergele
R = Rhyll
D = Dyserth
CM = Chat Moss
N = Nantwich
S = Stafford

Steaming into the North West
Tales of the Premier Line

1 – The Anxious Stoker (May 1832)

The two men were relaxing as far as their shaking, rattling, smoking steed - an 0-2-2 named *Phoenix* - allowed; they had taken the 40 or so passengers out of the Manchester terminus and were now passing the little village of Eccles. They were already travelling faster than any horse-drawn post-chaise, although a King's Messenger on a fast horse would have been able to match them at least for a few miles. But, thought Jeremy Hawthorne, pausing with his shovel in his hand and observing the passing scenery, the rider would soon have to give the horse a break if it were to survive, whereas on the train they could keep their speed up until they reached Liverpool, more than 30 miles away. Jeremy found his new job stimulating, and was proud of the fact that he was now employed by the Liverpool and Manchester Railway Company, which was able to take 2000 passengers a day between the two large cities; no stage coach company could match that!

But the approaching dark clouds evaporated his smugness; they were going to get very wet. The speed of the train would ensure that he would get far wetter than any stage coach driver would. Although Driver Sanders wore an overcoat, Jeremy found that any kind of coat hampered his work and he had to make do with a cap, which he now proceeded to tie on firmly to prevent it from blowing away.

In the train, the Second Class passengers, sitting on their wooden benches, hurriedly wrapped their coats and shawls around themselves. The slightly better financially-advantaged put on their waterproofs. Others simply prepared themselves for a soaking. Some Second Class carriages at least had a roof, but very little side protection from the weather, so passengers could expect plenty of rainwater to make its way inside.

In First Class, the well-to-do passengers could ignore the weather, albeit with the accompanying remarks expected at such times. Although the First Class carriages were far more efficiently equipped as regards weather protection, being in their design akin to three stage coach bodies on one base, the luggage on top had no such defence. But British weather, which had so horrified the Roman armies 2000 years earlier, did not worry modern Britons; they were inured to it. Indeed, railway passengers were generally pleased with this new mode of travel; it provided a remarkably frequent service, it was fast, and, above all, there was no need to worry about highwaymen, the bugbear of stage coach journeys.

Nevertheless, Jeremy wondered whether it would be possible for the designers to construct some sort of shelter for the crew of an engine; they were rather more exposed to the weather than a well-wrapped stage coach driver, sitting down on his run and not moving and turning about, shovelling coal. Still, he mused, at least when there was an icy blast from the north in winter, the firebox could provide a modicum of relief. Jeremy grabbed the edge of the coal box as the engine ran over a badly-laid length of track and shook itself like a dog after a swim.

His musings were interrupted by Driver Sanders, who had noticed the thoughtful expression on his mate's face: "What's on yer mind, Jeremy?"

"I was jus' thinkin' about 'ow there's no weather protection on these engines. Even stage coach drivers don't 'ave to put up with what we do at our speeds. Then there's all them sparks an' smoke an' steam all over yer face. Last year we 'ad the *Manchester* wot 'ad the tender in front an' I 'ad ter stand shovellin' the coal d'rekly under the chimney; I got meself covered in soot an' me 'at got burnt from they sparks."

"Is that what it is? Ah well, ye're not thinkin' right," said the driver, "we ain't like 'orsemen. Think o' sailors; take the topmen, f'rexample."

"Topmen? Me dad took me to a topping once; I din't like to see the poor buggers when they put the black cloths over their 'eads. They was screamin' an' kickin' before they stopped an' just 'ung there."

"No, I mean the sailors 'oo have to climb right to the top o' the masts in gales and storms to furl the sails in dirty weather. They don't 'ave much weather protection, neither!"

Jeremy shivered; "Even talkin' about that makes me privits freeze."

"Or yer could always go down a coal mine. No rain or wind down there!"

"No, but thousands o' tons o' rock above yer 'ead wot sometimes falls on yer."

"If yer don't like the weather, then tek my advice: go and learn yer letters and become a clerk in a hoffice."

"Me cousin's a clerk; he sez 'is boss is a miser and won't warm the office in winter, so Geoff allus 'as a blue 'ooter in winter."

Driver Sanders laughed; "Well, what sort of job d'yer want? Most people of our class these days are farm workers out in the weather all the year round, in cold offices or sheds with no 'eatin' and with long hours, workin' with transport 'orses inside or outside, or in the army or navy with daft officers, poor food and gettin' shot at."

"Aye, well I s'pose drivin' a train's about normal if yer think about it like that."

"Yeah, an' the pay's a bloody sight better'n wot others are gettin'. Now we're coming to a bit of a slope, so get shovellin' again so I can 'ave enough steam!"

In the 1830s, engine driving was a most unusual skill and was well paid compared to other jobs open to the lower classes. It didn't require any significant educational standards but it called for men with a highly developed mechanical instinct; such special skills were more highly prized and the men were paid accordingly.

They carried on up the slope and picked up speed down the other side and round a slight curve, until Driver Sanders suddenly swore and shouted, "Get the brake on, Jeremy! There's a bloody 'erd o' cattle on the line ahead!" The engine had no brakes but there was a lever attached to a wooden brake block, which applied pressure to a wheel of the tender.

Some of the carriages had a brakeman sitting high at the back in the open, where they could see the engine crew and wind the brake blocks onto the wheels if required. There were three of them at intervals along the train. Driver Sanders sounded the whistle urgently to warn them, and all three frantically wound their brakes on but, just when it seemed as if the train would inevitably plough into the herd of cows, a sheepdog shot around to head most of the animals off the track. There were two cows, however, who appeared determined to commit suicide and they dodged the dog's nipping jaws, carrying on their trot along the track, heading straight for the oncoming train.

The squealing of the brakes increased and the cows paused in their headlong trot, wondering what was making such a frightening noise. But whether it was the shrieking brakes or the outpouring of clouds of smoke which caused them to stop, toss their horns in disgust and turn off the track, Jeremy was not sure. With his sigh of relief and muttered swearing from his driver, they passed by the cattle with only a yard to spare. The train had slowed down considerably, which allowed one irate Second Class passenger to lean out of the carriage and smack the nearest cow with his walking stick as they passed the herd.

The cowherd saw this and the ensuing altercation between him and the angry passenger was such that a shocked mother in the carriage immediately seized her son's head and clapped her hands round his ears in case he should hear (and later employ) selected items of the vocabulary involved.

"They're goin' ter 'ave ter teach the farmers ter keep their stock out o' the way of our trains, Mr Sanders," commented Jeremy as they began to pick up speed once more. "Aye, they'll learn soon enough when they've lost a few cows, or the company'll 'ave to fence off the railway tracks. That'll cost 'em plenty and they won't like doin' that, neither," replied his driver, continuing ruefully, "Till then, you an' me will 'ave ter just watch out, and probably get the blame any'ow, for any cattle killed."

Arriving at the Crown Street terminus in Liverpool, Jeremy watched the passengers leaving the train with some difficulty, jostling the people waiting, who were trying to board quickly to grab the best seats. With some passengers still trying to leave and others fighting to get into the carriages, there was chaos on the carriages and the ground.

Those with luggage were having a particularly hard time as they fought for their cases, bags, parcels, and even cages of animals. There were also, Jeremy was sure, a few opportunistic characters whose major interest consisted of using the complete disorder to relieve travellers of their possessions. But suggesting to the few guardians of law and order that an arrest might be a good idea was a pointless exercise; any burden of proof would be very difficult to establish. In any case, catching a thief under the crowded circumstances in the station grounds would be almost impossible. Travellers clearly had a lot to learn about this new mode of transport.

Their engine backed out of the station in order to reach the engine shop and turntable, to be checked and refuelled ready for the return journey to Manchester on a later train.

"Are yer gettin' used ter this new duty then, Jeremy?" Driver Sanders enquired as they paused over their mugs of tea while waiting with their engine. "'Ave you thought of a better job?"

"Yer comments about sailors, Mr Sanders, 'ad me thinkin'; it must be a terrible job up the masts in a storm. I'd rather be on dry land after all. The bad weather we sometimes 'ave ter put up with is nowt really, we don't 'ave problems with 'ighwaymen, we get to travel between two great cities, and I think I can usually shovel the coal carefully into the firebox. But I've nearly been chucked off more'n once on a bad bit o' track. But I reckon I'll manage."

Driver Sanders smiled. "The shakin' don't bother yer then?"

"Not really; I know that the rails are sittin' on miles o' solid ground under them, so that meks me feel better! I 'ave a thing about solid ground; as a young sprog, I were once nearly taken by some quicksand, and since then I've allus wanted solid ground under me feet."

"Solid ground under yer feet, eh?" said Mr Sanders as a mischievous thought occurred to him; "'Ow about goin' over a bridge with a river below us?"

"Yeah well, I don't like that much neither, but yer past it afore yer know it."

On their return trip later that day, five miles out of Manchester, Driver Sanders eyed his stoker and said with a grin, "You wasn't 'appy without solid ground under yer feet, yer said?"

"Yeah, I like ter know I'm on safe ground."

"'Ow d'yer feel about 'avin' 35-foot o' bog under yer?"

"Cor, Mr Sanders, don't say things like that!"

"Yer didn't know, then?"

"Know wot?"

"At this very moment we're drivin' over Chat Moss, one o' the biggest an' deepest bogs in the north of England. When they built this 'ere line, they 'ad to lay a floatin' raft o' logs 30-foot deep and put the track on top of 'em."

Jeremy stared at his driver in horror; "Yer mean we're drivin' over a raft 'o logs now?"

"S'right!"

"Oh Cripes!"

2 - The Risk-Taker (November 1843)

Ned Houston was lazy. There was little question about this. He was also an unhappy man; his work on the farm had bored him. Farm work required hard physical labour, whereas he believed (erroneously) that his forte lay in a more cerebral field. He tried to join a haulage contractor but found that the bookwork was done by an older (and more diligent) clerk. The driving was admittedly not as difficult as farm labour but he had no affinity with the horses. Work in a village bakery had earned him enough to pay the rent in a cheap boarding house, but the amenities were disgusting, and there was only enough money left over for an occasional ale in the local pub.

Ned decided to travel to the nearby town of Crewe and try his luck there. He travelled by one of the new-fangled 'railways', as they were called, and on the journey he realised he had found the kind of work he might enjoy. As an engine driver, all you had to do was stand behind the engine and move a couple of levers, leaving the hard shovelling to the junior stoker on the footplate.

On his arrival at the station in Crewe, Ned saw a notice advertising work for 'men of some education' and, as his schooling had ensured that he was able to read, he applied immediately. He was a personable young man and had a letter of recommendation from his old headmaster.

The subsequent interview with the official was satisfactory and he was appointed to assist in workshop duties at the Crewe engine shop of the Grand Junction Railway.

Ned's introduction to the work in the first instance was eye-opening; he found himself surrounded by a variety of steam locomotives and, although the work in the shop required long hours and was often dirty and menial, that did not worry him because he knew that once he was on the footplate as a driver, the heavy work would be over for the rest of his life. He was intelligent enough to see how he could, once in a while, simplify a job or, to be more accurate, get others to do the heavy work while he found a seemingly complex duty which required the attention of a person of some education. His apparent ability was noticed by some of his more senior workmates and he was encouraged to take a greater interest in the technical details of the workings of the steam locomotive.

The locomotives of the Grand Junction Railway were bought from private contractors and varied in both reliability and quality. Repairing them often required the use of muscle so Ned applied for and received a transfer to the locomotive shed, where he believed he could work on an eventual career move to the position of Driver. He accepted that he would have to undertake some hard physical labour before he could achieve his aim.

In the shed, doing a variety of cleaning and sundry other jobs, Ned's interest in steam locomotive working was such that he was sometimes taken on the footplate when engines were moved about. He was shown the basics of how to fire the engine, and why the steam had to be kept up to pressure, thus allowing the locomotive to haul its load. He admired the polished wooden laths laid along the boiler of some locomotives and was told that the steel bands around them were designed to prevent the boilers exploding if the pressure became too great.

"We've got the safety valves, o' course," said one driver, "but sometimes-" and he lowered his voice here, "-we 'ave to 'old 'em down, otherwise they blow off and we can't get enough pressure to do the job."

"How do you do that?" Ned asked curiously.

"Ahh, that'd be tellin'," answered the driver with a grin, tapping the side of his nose. "I can't tell yer that, it ain't allowed."

"Isn't that dangerous, then?"

"Aye, it is a bit, but yer gets ter know the little tricks, like, and yer knows when ter loosen the valves."

"What happens if you don't loosen them?"

The driver laughed. "Simple – yer engine explodes! But don't worry – yer not goin' ter know much about it – yer'll be in a 'undred bits."

As time passed, Ned found himself taken on short journeys to and from Crewe, and once as far as Stafford. He learned the road to Newton Junction, where the GJR joined the Liverpool and Manchester Railway. On occasions, he was allowed to fire the engine of a goods train a few miles on the line to Chester, with a stoker watching his progress. Gradually, he developed some expertise at firing and as his skill developed he was allowed to fire on more straightforward turns for longer distances.

Life at Crewe was busy for Ned and he put up with the firing duties, developing a greater confidence on the footplate with a firm belief that promotion to Driver for a man of his skill could not be far off. But his frustration began to grow as he was only very rarely allowed on the regulator, and only then within the confines of the shed sidings. He was yet to learn that this relatively new mode of transport had its share of learning experiences, some of which could have dire consequences if not taken seriously.

One morning, Ned had fired an engine on a shed road, ready for departure to pick up its train, when Driver Joseph Heckmondwike realised that he had left his lunch behind. He went to fetch it and asked Ned to look after the engine; an old Bury 2-2-0, which had been at work for some eight years and was well past its best. The footplate was no longer quite straight and had a few rusted patches; several of the boiler laths needed replacing; steam was leaking out of a couple of places, and one cab side rail was out of shape and loose. The engine was to move out and couple up to a train of general merchandise to be taken to Manchester.

Ned had often been on such a simple manoeuvre and knew how it was done so he thought he could save his driver a bit of work and simultaneously demonstrate that he was perfectly capable of a basic driving task. If this was done properly he thought Driver Heckmondwike would be far more likely to recommend him for promotion to Driver, perhaps even in the near future.

He drove the engine slowly and carefully across the points to where the wagons were waiting, backing it down and gently stopping it where he could easily couple the tender to the waiting train of wagons. He then applied the brake to the tender, climbed down and lifted the hook and the safety chains on the first wagon, then hooked them up to the tender. That done, he mounted the footplate once more and, lifting the regulator gently, he waited for the train to move. The engine remained stationary.

Ned frowned; perhaps the pressure was not yet high enough to pull the train. He pushed another few shovels of coal into the boiler, but still the engine refused to move. He recalled a ploy about tightening the safety valve to increase the pressure. He knew that this was something that only experienced enginemen did, but as he felt himself to be close to becoming a competent driver, he believed he was justified in taking the risk. He did not think he could do much harm to the old engine if he was careful, and he also knew that Joe Heckmondwike was a kindly man who would not say or do anything to harm Ned's future prospects. Ned would be unlikely to be sacked by the shed foreman if anything went wrong. In this latter belief, he was perfectly correct.

As Ned considered the matter, a fitter went past him with a bag of tools and Ned called out to him.

The fitter stopped. "What?"

"Could I borrow your big spanner for a couple of minutes?"

"What for?"

"The pressure's too low and I want to tighten the safety valve a little."

"The safety valve? That's a dangerous procedure, young Houston, I'd leave that to yer driver, if I was you."

"Yes, of course. He's just gone to get his lunch, but with your spanner here, he'll be able to do the job more quickly and get this train away on time. I'll make sure you get your spanner back."

The fitter nodded and handed over the spanner. "I'll be back in fifteen minutes, and I'll want the spanner for me next job by then."

"My driver'll be back long before that and I'll get the spanner back to you."

The fitter walked away and disappeared round the back of the train. Ned waited until the fitter was well out of sight before he climbed onto the boiler, took the spanner to the safety valve, and tightened it slightly. Climbing back to the footplate, he tried the regulator again; this time, the engine shuddered gently but did not move. He wondered whether to climb back and tighten the valve a little once more but paused, puzzled as to why the locomotive was so reluctant to move. All at once, he realised that he had omitted to release the tender brake. That was it!

As he turned to the tender to take its brake off, the locomotive boiler exploded, snapping the boiler bands and scattering its protective laths across a wide area. In some nearby trees, a flock of crows roosting took to the air in fright, cawing loudly in protest, and the explosion woke a tramp who had been asleep in a wagon on a nearby siding. The locomotive's right-hand driving wheel was blown off the frame and clean through the wooden wall of the shed. Parts of the safety valve were later discovered 150 yards away.

None of these problems were of concern to Ned Houston, however. The force of the explosion had snapped off the fire door and sent it spinning like a top. It had hit Ned's spine, almost separating his torso from the lower half of his body, and a large lump of burning coal had shattered the left-hand side of his head.

A later investigation of his corpse showed that while most of his injuries could be explained by the explosion, his uninjured feet were missing both shoes. This puzzled the coroner greatly as there was no obvious explanation. In fact, the tramp had found the body first and had used the opportunity to acquire the footwear, even though the shoes didn't fit him very well. He packed them with some grass and stole unobtrusively from the scene.

Engineers examining the remains of the engine saw that the metal in the boiler remnants had worn down to less than an eighth of an inch thick in places and, further, many of the bolts on the frames had worn loose. Regular checking of old engines had obviously been lax, and the wear on the old boiler had not been noticed.

This infant transport industry was clearly still at the beginning of its learning curve regarding safety and careful maintenance of its rolling stock.

3 - The Pugnacious Clerk (October 1848)

Dennis Hignett was a big man who enjoyed partaking in a spot of fisticuffs from time to time. He could make a few extra shillings on market-day evening if he wasn't working on the railway, and he enjoyed the feeling of laying out an opponent flat in the dirt. If there was blood to be seen, then all the better.

Admittedly, it cost him a bruise or two now and again, but the sight of a groaning man on the ground and the florins in his hand were an adequate recompense for the minor injuries. Yet curiously, in spite of this, Dennis was no bully; he only fought those who were willing to take him on. He had no time for others who used their size and weight simply to cow their fellow men or beat their womenfolk. He generally got on well with his mates in the Shrewsbury and Chester Railway and was known to be polite to passengers at the Chester joint railway station, where he worked as a clerk selling tickets, advising passengers about train times and possible connections with trains of neighbouring companies.

As a lowly clerk, Dennis was not involved in the high politics of the various railway companies of the day, but he was concerned at any inconvenience and annoyance caused to his passengers and regarded with increasing dismay the constant quarrelling between his company, the Chester & Holyhead Railway, and the Chester & Birkenhead Railway; the three companies which jointly owned the station.

His station at this time was anything but a pleasant place to work; it was the centre of an incipient battlefield. The C & H and the C&B were both under the thumb of the mighty London and North Western Railway, which had recently been formed out of the amalgamation of the Grand Junction, London & Birmingham, and the Liverpool & Manchester Railways, with additional smaller railways which had been bought out. Indeed, the Chester & Holyhead Railway did not own any railway vehicles and leased all its rolling stock from the LNWR. The problem had originally arisen when the little Shrewsbury & Chester railway had formed a legal agreement with the Chester & Birkenhead Railway to transport passengers and goods to Birkenhead from the south. This now provided a speedier alternative route from the Midlands to the port of Birkenhead, thus removing the LNWR's monopoly of traffic from the south, and this the LNWR found intensely annoying. The whole matter was exacerbated by a movement from the Oxford & Birmingham Railway to link up with the Shrewsbury companies. Behind this move, the LNWR suspected that its rival, the huge Great Western Railway (which had strong influence over the S&B), was planning to reach the port of Birkenhead with its controversial broad gauge. They were not wrong.

The LNWR could not legally deny use of the Birkenhead tracks to the 'Fighting Shrewsburys' (as the Shrewsbury & Chester and the Shrewsbury & Birmingham companies were sometimes known) and neither could they prevent Shrewsbury passengers from reaching Birkenhead; both agreements were legally tight, and the attempts to break them were fought tooth-and-nail by the Shrewsbury companies. The LNWR tried to force their allied companies to undercut the Shrewsbury companies' freight rates, to discourage the carriage of goods by hostile companies from the south.

But when the C&S retaliated and began to unload their goods at Saltney to wagons for Birkenhead and the Mersey, this was the straw that broke the camel's back and the situation developed into all-out war. Trade quarrels between the railway companies in Britain were fairly common as companies tried to increase their earning capacity, but it was rare (though by no means unknown) for them to actually take the law into their own hands.

One morning, as Dennis came to his office in Chester station, he found Frank Powlett and two other beefy C&B railwaymen standing by his door, apparently intent on opposing his entry.

"Morning, lads," said Dennis with a smile on his face, "was there something you wanted?"

"Yes, Dennis," replied Frank, "we'd like you to turn round and go home again."

"Now why would I want to do that?" Dennis asked, noting with surprise that a small C&B 0-4-2 engine was occupying the platform which an S&C train was due to enter. "And what's that Birkenhead engine doing on our platform?"

"Simple enough, Dennis; your Shrewsbury trains are taking a lot of our traffic away from us. We can't have that!"

"What we're doing is perfectly legal; many railways compete with each other for business. What's wrong with that? Now you'll oblige me by standing away from the door to my office."

Frank didn't move. "Now, now, Dennis, don't get hasty; you just go home like a good lad and leave us to explain to any passengers who want to book their tickets here about the changed arrangements."

"What changed arrangements?"

"If they've booked through from the south to Birkenhead, they will need to rebook here."

"What, and pay twice?"

The C&B man shook his head. "Of course not; we're not thieves. If they want to travel from Shrewsbury to Birkenhead, they just need to travel with the London and North Western via Crewe."

"But that takes much longer; our way is far quicker."

"Yes, that is a bit unfortunate; but now move away, Dennis, we can't stay arguing all day."

Dennis decided that enough was enough. "When my boss tells me the arrangements have been changed, I'll do what he says. Now, Frank, move away from my door, before I move you myself."

Frank, who should have known better, leaned forward and seized Dennis's right hand. This was an error: Dennis was ambidextrous and he shot out his left hand, grabbed Frank by the throat, and threw him aside. Frank's two companions immediately moved in to the fight but neither, it seemed, were used to brawling, and soon they too were picking themselves up from the ground where they had found themselves, and retired from the fray.

In the meantime, the Shrewsbury train was approaching the station. Its driver caught sight of the C&B engine on his platform. He turned to his mate on the footplate. "I heard that there might be trouble here, Sid," he said, "Looks like it's arrived!"

"What'll you do, Mr Kemp?"

"I'm going to push that little engine right up to the stop blocks. We've got a bigger engine and the whole weight of our train; it can't argue with that!"

He continued into the platform and up to the C&B engine, which he forced backwards, its brakes unable to combat the weight and inertia of the arriving train, until there was enough room for his passengers to alight. The C&B engine was now firmly locked in, with the stop blocks behind it and the Shrewsbury train blocking its exit.

"Let's see what they do about that, then," said Driver Kemp in satisfaction to his mate Sid Green, as they settled and began to eat their packed lunch.

They soon found out.

A pair of heavy C&B 0-6-0 engines, coupled together, were gently easing over the points to their platform, and before Driver Kemp and his mate could drop their lunch and move their train out of the trap, their own exit was blocked.

In the meantime, the Chester & Birkenhead company had been busy elsewhere; a large group of hired bruisers had entered the Chester & Shrewsbury premises in the station and broken down the door to Dennis Hignett's office. Dennis put up a fierce resistance and two of the bruisers finished up on the floor, one out for the count and the other holding his broken arm.

"I'll have the peelers onto the lot of you!" shouted Dennis as he was held by four of the men while two others amused themselves by punching him around the head. He was then frogmarched out onto the road outside, while others seized armfuls of the tickets and timetables and threw them into the road. Dennis found himself prone with a bloodied face (a situation he himself had put more than one opponent into), surrounded by a litter of paper.

"Now then, Dennis lad," said one of his attackers, "next time, take advice when it's kindly given!" With that parting shot, they left him sitting in the road among his tickets. His fellow Shrewsbury men, Driver Kemp and Sid Green, came to his assistance, but there was little else they could do to help.

However, when the Chester & Birkenhead management gleefully informed their LNWR colleagues that the threat from the south had been checkmated, they were premature. The two Shrewsbury companies and their Great Western allies called in their lawyers. These were able to convince the court that the original agreements for the through bookings from the south to Birkenhead could not be broken. Clerk Hignett was able to return to his office in Chester station and resume his duties without hindrance.

Curiously, after the various railway companies had settled their differences and reached a compromise, the GWR and the LNWR (and later the WR and LMR) managed to jointly run the Chester & Birkenhead route amicably for the next 150 years. The LNWR lost their monopoly from the south, and although the GWR won their route to Birkenhead, they lost their chance of extending their broad gauge, as the Shrewsbury railways had never contemplated using it and had not allowed for it in building their tracks.

Dennis Hignett, on the other hand, had no intention of working amicably with his clerical colleagues of the Birkenhead railway. But his valiant (though unsuccessful) defence of his office had been observed by a senior official of the S&C, who had put his name forward to represent the company in a railway boxing competition. This time there was a happier result and he won the official prize of £200 - a fortune for a lowly clerk.

Yet he was still bitter at the beating he had received; he had recognised several of the men during the altercation and felt that while one-to-one was a fair fight, they needed to be shown that one against six did not accord with the spirit of seemliness (to be codified some 20 years later under the aegis of the Marquess of Queensberry), and retribution was therefore called for.

Frank Powlett was walking home in the late evening from the pub when he was stopped by a voice; "Well now, if it isn't Mr Powlett having an evening stroll. Just the man I wanted a word with!"

Frank turned to see a burly man in the gloom.

"Who's that?" he asked.

"Never mind, Frank," said the other, "you're going the wrong way!"

"No, I'm going to my bed."

"Your bed's that way," said the burly man, pointing down a side road.

"That's only the way to the hospital," pointed out Frank.

"Yes," came the reply, accompanied by a heavy clout to the head. Frank fell down and felt several kicks to his ribs, which broke two of them.

By the end of the month, a number of Frank's colleagues had also suffered evening attacks. Yet complaints to Sir Robert Peel's new police force of the brutality of Clerk Hignett were unavailing: he could not possibly have been involved. At each time stated, he had been in an inn at Saltney, enjoying a beer with his two friends, Mr Kemp and Mr Green.

4 - The Angry Lieutenant (November 1854)

The troop train along the route of the Chester & Holyhead Railway was a heavy one and kept Fireman Don Hampton busy on the shovel as the train pitched and swayed on its journey along the coast to Holyhead. Replacement troops were needed in Ireland, to replace those who had been sent to the Crimea; the Russians were putting up heavier resistance than the Allied armies of the British, French and Turks had expected. National governments were rapidly discovering that the railways were an excellent method of transporting large numbers of troops quickly, and with relative ease, over long distances.

The situation in the Crimea was becoming chaotic; Sebastopol was strongly defended and holding out against the besieging armies and the Allies were losing far more men from disease and, unfortunately, sheer military incompetence than from enemy action. Furthermore, a new dimension to government problems was arising: the newspapers had been sending war correspondents to the scenes of battle and they reported what they saw in frequently embarrassing detail. Exposure of military failures was getting much harder to censor and the reading public was causing concern in a Parliament which had, after the Reform Act of 1832, a somewhat greater sense of responsibility among its MPs to their constituencies. In short, the population in Britain was more aware of what its government was doing and quite prepared to do something about it at the next election.

But the social situation in Ireland, due to the disastrous potato famine of 1845-52, was still uneasy; many blamed absentee English landlords, who were often uncaring about the welfare of their tenants. The tenants themselves usually had plots of land so small that they could only subsist on the potato. When the blight had occurred they had lost their sole subsistence food. Consequently, thousands of them starved.

None of these matters occupied Don Hampton's mind as he continued shovelling the coal into the ever-hungry firebox of the 2-2-2 express, one of the LNWR engines. The LNWR supplied the rolling stock of the Chester & Holyhead Railway and was shortly to incorporate the little railway company into its own conglomeration. Don glanced at his driver, Mr Simkin, who was a taciturn man although not by any means unfriendly. The driver noticed the glance and nodded; he looked up at the sky, shaking his head.

Don looked up too and grumbled, "Looks like we'll be getting very wet soon."

The low, dark clouds were approaching fast and the first drops already landing on their faces. The ever-present headwind was taxing the little engine and causing the raindrops to sting the faces of the crew. For many miles, all the way from Point of Ayr as far as Bangor, the track ran along the North Wales coast, so neither man was unduly surprised; getting wet was a normal part of the day's work. Some town cab drivers could expect a roof over their heads but long-distance stage coach drivers and most locomotive crewmen had no protection from the weather besides whatever clothing they could provide for themselves. Most locomotives had no protection for their crews except a front-facing spectacle plate and either a side plate on the footplate or a simple handrail.

The rain was becoming heavy, blowing straight off the Irish Sea into their faces, making forward observation tricky. Both men kept a sharp lookout for the signals along the side of the tracks as they worked their engine. Driver Matthew Simkin, with great regret, eased the regulator and allowed the headwind to slow the train in order to give them a better chance to react to the signals if they showed danger; a risky business because it might affect their expected arrival time at Holyhead Admiralty Jetty. This in turn could have the result of the troopship missing the tide, which allowed the exit from the harbour, and thus affecting the arrival time at Dun Laoghaire. The telegraph connection, of course, would keep the authorities informed but it would still conceivably cause the loss of a whole day and would reflect badly on the C&HR. Blaming the weather would also not endear the train crew to railway management and that could be reflected in their next pay package.

But it was no use; the rain was now so heavy and the visibility so poor that Driver Simkin slowed the train almost to a stop as they approached the signal near Penmaenmawr, but it did not show anything. In fact, neither the disk nor the board was visible; both seemed to be missing from the mast altogether. They had to stop.

"Get down, Don, and find out from the bobby what's going on," said Driver Simkin. Men who operated the signals besides their rudimentary little huts were called bobbies, after Sir Robert Peel's police.

"I bet the bloody man's inside his hut, sheltering from the rain!"

growled Don, staring at the hut.

"Well, see what he's has to say for himself before we lose any more time." Matthew Simkin was getting seriously annoyed at the delay caused by an inconsiderate bobby; he should have been waiting outside for them, under company instruction, and he would have known they were due and should not be held up.

"Where are you, you lazy bugger?" Driver Simkin heard his fireman's angry shout as he entered the hut.

Don reappeared a few moments later and his face was pale as he climbed up onto the engine. "I think he's dead, Mr Simkin!" he gasped.

"What!"

"He's lying on the floor and not moving, and I couldn't feel any pulse! The disk and the board are lying next to him."

By this time, a young lieutenant, in his bright red coat and carrying an umbrella, had arrived at the engine. He addressed the two men furiously. "What the hell's the delay? We have a ship to catch!"

"I'm sorry, Sir, we cannot move forward until we ascertain that the track ahead is clear for us."

"Well, find out, man, double quick!"

"We cannot do that quickly, Sir; the man who can let us know seems to be dead."

"Christ! Then find someone who can tell you. What are you waiting for?"

Another officer, a major, arrived on the scene. "What's the delay, Mr Rogers, why have we stopped?"

"These drivers are incompetent, Sir, they have stopped the train and refuse to move it."

Driver Simkin addressed the senior officer: "With respect, Sir, your officer is mistaken. We are not refusing to move the train. We are merely following company rules that will not allow us to endanger our passengers by proceeding into a section that may already have another train in it. The only thing we can do under the circumstances is to move forward at such speed that we can stop in time if we see another train ahead of us. We must also report our dead bobby to the next section signalman. If you gentlemen will board the train once more, we can move off again."

The major grunted assent. "Hmm, very well. Rogers, have a stretcher-bearer put the dead man on the train, let the crew get the train moving again. Then we can all get out of this bloody rain."

"All very well for them, they can climb back into their nice dry carriage, while we carry on getting soaked," Don Hampton growled bitterly as they began to move off slowly, staring carefully ahead into the downpour.

At the next section hut, they halted to report the incident to the bobby who was waiting outside. Again, Lieutenant Rogers came out and angrily demanded the reason for this pause in their progress. Driver Simkin stared at him and asked, "What do you do when your major gives you an order?"

"I'm an army officer; I obey it, naturally!" he replied indignantly.

"Of course you do," responded the driver, "But enginemen also obey orders, and that's what we're doing!"

"But *I'm* giving you an order to get moving!"

Driver Simkin was getting rather tired of this ill-mannered young man. "You are not our superior officer! Now why don't you get back into your carriage and leave us to get on with our job? That way we will all get to Holyhead more quickly."

Lieutenant Rogers was clearly about to lose his temper when he glimpsed his major looking out of the carriage and retreated back into it. The signalman immediately telegraphed the details to Holyhead and the train was permitted to proceed at a more normal speed. Yet just as they began to make up lost time, the train jerked and began to accelerate rapidly. Don's shovelful of coal spilled onto the floor, and he looked back to see most of the train slowing down while they accelerated.

"Mr Simkin, the train's parted!" he shouted. Matthew Simkin turned around, startled to see that they only had three carriages attached; the rest of the train was already some 40 yards behind, and slowing down.

"Bugger!" shouted the driver, as he slowed the engine down once more.

"At least we're on the level," commented Don, "the carriages won't run on to us."

They stopped the train once again and Driver Simkin climbed down to walk back and check the couplings of the last carriage. The coupling hook and one side-chain had broken while the other side-chain was dangling loose.

He walked back to the first carriage of the rest of the train, which had by now trundled to a stop 100 yards back. As he suspected, the left-hand chain had snapped. He returned to the engine to find Lieutenant Rogers haranguing his fireman.

"You are holding up Her Majesty's army!" he was shouting. "This train with its 80 soldiers is going to be late! I am going to have you two sacked the moment we arrive in Holyhead!" Matthew Simkin spotted the major approaching and went over to him, totally ignoring the furious lieutenant.

"We have broken a coupling, Sir," he pointed out, "but rather than wait for assistance, could we perhaps use chains from one of your gun limbers to recouple the carriages?"

"I'm sure we can help you there, Driver." The major turned to the lieutenant, "Get some men, Rogers and have that seen to instead of blustering and wasting time!"

"Yessir!"

Fifteen minutes later, Driver Simkin had backed the engine, with its three carriages, onto the parted carriages and army engineers had managed to chain them together once more. He gingerly put the train back into motion, checking frequently to see whether the jury rig held. Arriving two hours late in Holyhead, they found the rest of the regiment waiting impatiently in the pouring rain.

A furious general officer rode up on his horse as the major climbed out of the train. "What in hell's been happening, Major Jackson? Why are you so damned late?"

"Not our fault, Sir, there were a couple of problems on the railway. Our engineers did a fine job making a temporary repair to-"

"Oh, don't give me any of your infernal excuses! Just get your men off the train and march them with the rest of the regiment onto the ship this instant!"

"Sir!"

As they watched the soldiers march down the platform where they could see the sails of a troopship awaiting them, Don Hampton shook his head. "In spite of us getting soaked and them in the dry carriages, I don't envy those poor buggers at all, Mr Simkin."

"Of course not, Don," Driver Simkin's words were soothing. "Still, I wouldn't like to be in the shoes of the Chester shunter who forgot to hook on both safety-chains between our carriages. The coupling hook broke and then, with only one chain between them, the strain of the snatch was too great. With both chains holding, the train might not have parted. That shunter has simply been very careless."

The Holyhead stationmaster came over to find the reason for the late arrival of the train.

"Not our fault at all, Sir," Driver Simkin replied, "the signal at Penmaenmawr had a missing disk and board and the bobby was dead, and it was impossible to decide whether it was safe for us to continue; then we had a broken coupling."

"I see, and what did you do?"

"We put the dead bobby in the brake van, and got some army engineers to make a temporary coupling so that we could continue."

The stationmaster nodded. "You did well. I'll expect a full report in an hour."

Matthew Simkin looked at his fireman again then smiled, "D'you still feel sorry for those soldiers, Don?"

Don Hampton nodded. "Indeed I do, Mr Simkin. Not only do the poor devils have to go and fight, but they've got officers with loud voices and a bullying nature! My grandpa served at Waterloo and from what he said, it was the same then, and I bet you a pound to a penny it'll be the same again in 1900!"

5 - The Hazardous Coast (May 1865)

Jerry Monmouth was an experienced driver who enjoyed his job and, furthermore, enjoyed the Crewe to Holyhead run, which was his regular shift. Trevor Mansfield, his fireman, however, was fairly new to the shift, having been a cleaner at Banbury in the LNWR's Southern Division. He had been transferred into the Northern Division based in Crewe and was getting used to his new duties. Trevor was showing both willingness and ability and his driver had confidence that he would make a competent fireman after he had gained a little more experience. But Jerry wondered how we would manage with the North Wales coast, which was a very different kettle of fish from the Banbury to Bletchley run that Trevor knew.

Between Crewe and Holyhead, there were no difficult hills to climb and there were also several straight stretches where a late train could get into its stride and make up lost time, but this did not mean that the run was always an easy one. Aside from the mostly minor failings of men and equipment – and the LNWR, like most railways of the time, was prone to many of these – there were also problems provided by the weather. Wind and rain along the coast could be savage at times, and empty vans blown clean off the tracks were by no means unknown.

Jerry and his mate had picked up their engine at Crewe shed and were to take over the Irish Mail train to Holyhead; it was brought in by one of the Southern Division's powerful 2-2-2 express engines (known to the railway fraternity as 'Bloomers' on account of the exposure of the underframes and big seven-foot driving wheels revealed below the footplate, after the daring female fashion of the day). The train was waiting on the main down platform while the engines were being changed over. Their engine was a 2-2-2 Lady class in its Northern division bluish-green. On the footplate there was scant protection for the crew, as it only had a spectacle plate and weatherboard with round windows; but Jerry and Trevor were quite used to this. Across the whole of Britain, few express engines had any greater protection for their crews. Designers apparently assumed that if a stage coach driver could manage in the fresh air, then so could engine crews; the fact that trains could travel much faster was not taken into account. Indeed, one medical expert vigorously insisted that any person travelling at over 40 miles an hour would inevitably suffer fatal brain damage, and the autocratic chairman of the LNWR, Sir Richard Moon, decreed that this was fast enough for any express train, the important Irish Mail being no exception.

The day was proving to be quite useful, Jerry thought, in giving his fireman a taste of what the North Wales coast was capable of. An up train driver had told him that the weather along the coast had been blustery. "We could be in for some excitement today, Trevor," he said to his mate.

"Excitement, Mr Monmouth? What sort of excitement?"

"Weather, lad, rain and wind. And what's more," Jerry added, "it'll be on your side of the footplate. Still, we can be thankful for the weatherboard, however small it might be."

"Yeah, I've got wet enough in Bletchley. Why don't they give us more protection from the weather, then?"

"I think that may be coming. I was in the works a few weeks back and saw a picture of a new Scottish engine with side sheets and even a roof."

"I like the sound of that. But what's so special about today's weather?"

"We'll get very wet, it could slow us down; you might be surprised how hard it can blow along the coast."

Trevor was sceptical; "Can't be worse than some of the weather we had in the Chilterns."

Jerry smiled, "Well, in an hour or so you'll be able to judge for yourself."

As they drove north-west along the Dee estuary towards Point of Ayr, Jerry could see that the word 'blustery' was underestimating what was to come. Curving round the west on the approach to Prestatyn, the wind had picked up and was now driving the rain horizontally straight across the tracks. Trevor, bending to throw a shovelful of coal into the firebox, lost his cap, which was whisked away across the fields at high speed. Instantly, his hair was soaked, and streamed rigidly out to his left. The footplate was becoming extremely uncomfortable and even Driver Monmouth was becoming unhappy with the conditions, even though they were unpleasantly familiar to him. His fireman was having a very rough time; the coal mostly went into the firebox, but plenty of lumps left the shovel and ended briefly on the footplate, where they were whisked away inland before Trevor could retrieve them.

Between Rhyl and Abergele, they passed an up goods train, whose enginemen appeared to be having equal difficulties managing, and the two crews didn't even have time to exchange the customary waves. Just after the goods had passed them, its final two wagons and the brake van pitched over and across the tracks which their own train had just left. Trevor had been turning for more coal from the tender and saw this. He yelled to his driver; "God's teeth, Mr Monmouth! The goods has just derailed behind us!"

Driver Monmouth also turned, saw the accident, and shouted, "We can't stop here, we'd be no use to them. We'll stop in Abergele and warn the stationmaster; he can send help. He'll warn the bobbies to ensure the section is protected." They drew in at Abergele, much to the anger of the stationmaster: "What the hell d'you think you're doing, Driver? The Mail is not allowed to stop here!"

"No, sir, I'm aware of that, but the rear three vehicles of the up goods have come off the track a mile or so back. We're not even sure whether the engine crew noticed, the weather is so bad. The poor guard may be badly injured. You will need to warn the bobbies and get an emergency crew to the site."

The shocked stationmaster nodded: "Oh, good God! I'll get help right away. Thank you for letting me know; but you get moving again and I'll note why you stopped against regulations – you won't be penalised."

"Thank you, sir." Jerry climbed back on his footplate straightaway and they set off once more.

The short pause had given both crewmen a breather from the weather but as soon as they moved off again they were struggling against the wind and rain once more. The foul weather followed them all the way to Bangor, where they were held up at the station as a small shunter's hut had been blown down across the tracks. The weather only began to ease once they were clear of Robert Stephenson's Britannia Bridge over the Menai Strait and into Anglesey, where, away from the coast, they were shielded from the worst of the storm. Yet even here it was raining heavily and giving the men very little respite. They were very relieved to know that were to stay overnight in Holyhead before returning with the up mail the following day. They hoped this would give the weather time to mend.

The next day was indeed a vast improvement, but they learned that they had not been the only footplatemen to suffer from the appalling weather; in fact, their own suffering was not yet over because a number of trains had been cancelled and, consequently, their load the next day was heavier than originally planned; three extra postal vans were added because the Irish mail boat had docked in the meantime. They saw three sorters climbing into the first van to begin sorting the letters for the journey.

"Sorry, Trevor me lad, I was hoping you would get an easier trip back today," commented Jerry, as they prepared to move out of the station, "but with the extra load and the same engine, you'll be shovelling hard again. I'll give you a hand whenever I can."

"Thanks, Mr Monmouth, but at least we won't have to fight the weather this time. That should make a big difference." The weather had improved dramatically, as though to atone for that of the previous day; the sunshine was considerably warmer.

On the platform, while they were waiting for the porters to load the last mailbags, they observed a little boy calling excitedly to an elderly lady sitting nearby on a bench: "Look, Naina, that's a Lady class injin!"

The elderly lady glanced at Driver Monmouth, who smiled and nodded at the lad's statement. She smiled fondly at her grandson: "Well, that's *clever* you are, Johnny bach!"

"Nice omen for the trip, Mr Monmouth," remarked Trevor as they gradually moved out of the station and up the gradient from the pier. But he soon began to feel that he might have been unduly optimistic: the train was very heavy and its climb up the hill was laboured. He was already shovelling hard by the time they were passing Trearddur, only a few miles out of Holyhead.

"Might have to stop in Bangor for a pilot engine, if they've got one," muttered Jerry; he had also noticed the way his locomotive was labouring with its additional load. But as they crossed the Britannia Bridge, he felt that his engine and young fireman had the measure of the train and they passed Bangor without having to stop to request assistance.

Only a few miles later, however, he was wondering whether his decision to continue as they were had been wise. They were not able to pick up any speed, in spite of the track being mostly level and Trevor's work on the shovel managing to keep up steam pressure. He consoled himself that either Rhyl shed or certainly Chester would be able to provide a pilot engine if need be, and there were no heavy gradients before they could sign off at Crewe.

Just before the great headland at Penmaenmawr, a down train passed them slowly; it too was a heavy train, as if to emphasize the LNWR's miserly attempts to compensate for the cancelled traffic of the previous day. Entering the long Penmaenbach tunnel, they were instantly smothered by the smoke left from the passed down train; this slowed them somewhat as the engine's fire, starved of fresh air, began to die down. It got worse as their own smoke added to that which was already lingering in the tunnel, and before they had gone more than halfway, they were both crouching to try and breathe the lower-down air, which was only slightly less smoky.

The engine struggled on but soon both men were lying flat on their footplate, their faces as low as they could get them, with the hope that the train would make it to the end of the 700-yard tunnel. Finally, it crawled out and the men at their last gasp were able to breathe easily once more. They spent a few moments simply coughing out the smoke from their lungs.

"Ye gods, Trevor, I've been in smoky tunnels before, but that was one of the worst!"

"Any more tunnels like that?" Trevor was shaken.

"A couple of short ones at Chester but no, nothing like that before Crewe, thank heaven."

"What about the sorters in the postal vans?"

"If they've had any sense, they'll have closed all doors and windows fast before we entered the tunnel, and then opened up again; but we'd better stop and make sure."

Once well clear of the tunnel, they drew to a halt and opened the door of the first postal van. Three men lay on the floor inside; two of them were gasping as smoke drifted out and fresh air flowed in. The third man did not move.

"Get that cove to the door, quick, Trevor!" called the driver, pointing to the prone sorter.

Trevor hauled the man to the door and slapped his face a couple of times; the other two gradually shook themselves and stood up shakily. One of them went over to his mate by the door and called to him, "Hoy, wake up, Art!"

But in spite of their attention, the man did not move.

Post Office Sorter Arthur Dixon was dead.

6 - The Ailing Signalman (August 1883)

It was one of those days when merely being an engine driver taking a fast train was nothing less than a simple delight. The weather was pleasant, with a gentle sun and a slight breeze; the coal was well broken up so that Jeffrey Harding, Matthew's fireman, didn't have to break any lumps while firing; and the engine, one of Mr Webb's new 2-4-0s, was purring along nicely. Even the signals seemed to be agreeable, allowing them to pass without hindrance.

Driver Matthew Bolton knew this run extremely well as he and Fireman Harding had made it countless times already; Euston to Carlisle was the premier line on the London and North Western Railway. The drop down the Lake District hills towards Carlisle, where the Caledonian Railway could take over the Glasgow trains, was, in Matthew's opinion, the most satisfactory stretch of the line; they could relax after the hard slog to Tebay and then over the top at Shap. This had long been the hardest run on the west coast main line and the LNWR chief mechanical engineers had been hard pressed to produce a locomotive which could tackle it with a heavy train and still maintain timing. Now, it seemed, they had one; these Precedents appeared to be the enginemen's answer, although with the continuing increase in train weights it was still a question of how long they would suit.

Driver Bolton was a tall, rather gangly, figure, with an apparent hesitation in his movements that seemed to imply an insecurity in his work. He was, it has to be admitted, an unusually ugly man: his lips were rather thick, and his slightly elongated head and protruding ears added to the impression that he need not be taken seriously. But such a conclusion from any casual observer would be entirely in error; in fact, Matthew was completely at ease in his work and always knew exactly what he was doing. He just didn't rush his actions. He was also well aware that his appearance gave rise to amusement among those who didn't know him, yet this didn't bother him in the slightest. His home life was happy, although many men wondered how it was that such an attractive woman (as his wife Elsie unquestionably was) could possibly see anything in him. But they did not realise what most women knew instinctively: although a good-looking man may have an immediate superficial attraction, physical appearance was a highly unreliable guide to his worth as a long-term partner. Elsie had been entirely satisfied with her choice for well over 40 years.

Jeff Harding looked up from his firing and turned to his driver. "We should be right now, Matt, for the last run in to Carlisle."

"Fine, Jeff, you can relax a bit now." They both enjoyed these last few miles in to Carlisle. Rolling in on time to the big, imposing station where half-a-dozen railway companies met never failed to provide a sense of achievement.

The Caledonian engine backed on to their coaches, ready to take them further on to Scotland. In the meantime, Matt and Jeff backed their engine to Upperby shed for servicing and turning, ready for the return journey. They had several hours to spare and sat in the enginemen's mess to enjoy their tea and sandwiches, and listen to the gossip about their new chief engineer Mr George Whale, a man of considerable experience.

The night was warm and there were still no clouds in the sky when the two enginemen climbed back into their engine to back up to Carlisle Citadel Station, ready to take their train back to Crewe, where a Camden crew would take it on to Euston. The locomotive had been serviced and cleaned for them, the coal looked as if it had been specially sorted, and even the cab interior looked as if it had received a cleaner's attention. Extra care had been taken today because they were to have 'a personage of some considerable importance' on board; that was all they had been told, but the attention of senior officials had alerted them to something unusual about their train.

While Jeff climbed down to couple the engine to the coaches, which the Caley engine had brought in on time, Matt kept an eye open as the passengers passed him along the platform; one attractive young lady he noticed, presumably one of the quality, was accompanied by two soberly dressed men, one on either side of her, and two policemen sauntered past, keeping an eye on the crowd. That was not normal in Carlisle. Passengers here were more concerned with checking for their connecting trains than getting involved in antisocial disturbances.

Jeff climbed back into the cab, nodding towards the young lady and grinning at his driver; "That's one o' the Prince's doxies, Matt."

"How do you know that?"

"Easy! A pretty girl with a locked compartment provided for 'er an' four coppers with 'er? What else would she be?"

"I only saw two coppers."

"Nah, there were two more but they weren't in uniform; they were bodyguards, I'd say."

Matt nodded. Jeff knew what he was talking about; he had been an orphan and had been on the streets since he was ten, and seen the inside of a nick more than once. He had been a clever pickpocket until he had tried it on with someone he had assumed to be an unsuspecting punter at Ascot. The punter had in fact been a detective on the lookout for pickpockets, and Jeff had done two years before joining the London & North Western Railway. He had never tried to hide his past and had been firing with Driver Bolton for almost 20 years now.

The young lady who had been the subject of the discussion was whisked with her two companions into the extra coach, and the policemen left the platform to its normal respectability.

"Seems as if we're to have another good run this morning, Jeff," commented Matthew. The train was quite heavy and the Caley crew had done well to get into Carlisle on time over the Scottish hills. The Precedent pulled away easily with the train and Jeff put several shovelfuls of coal where he thought they were needed, ready for the hard pull up into the hills south of Carlisle.

"You could be right about this trip, Matt!" Jeff's voice reflected his cheerful mood, "The Glasgow blokes have given us a good start and we should be able to get into Crewe bang on time."

The two crewmen were not to know that their optimism was to be tragically unwarranted.

Far to the south in the hills, the night duty signalman was having a very unpleasant shift; his daughter was seeing a young man neither he nor his wife approved of, and he had quarrelled with his wife about what to do about it. His shift predecessor in the box had left the place in a filthy mess and, to cap it all, the signalman had a severe cold. He was making himself a cup of tea with a sly slug of rum in it when there was a knock on his door.

"What the hell?" The startled signalman spilled his tea before hurrying to the door and opening it.

A farmer stood there. "Some dozy bugger's left a gate open an' me bloody sheep are all over yer railway line! Yer'll 'ave ter stop the trains!"

Swearing, the signalman set both the up and down signals to 'stop', to prevent any trains from entering the section.

"How long before you get your sheep off our railway?" he demanded, "We can't stop the trains very long."

"I'll do me best," called the farmer, "it'll tek me nobbut fifteen minutes. I'll shout an' knock when they're away." And he hurried off to round up his sheep.

Ten minutes later there was a tap on the window. "Must have got his sheep off the tracks," muttered the signalman to himself and, assuming the line was clear once more, he went back to finish drinking his tea and making up his train diary.

Unfortunately, the tap on the window had not been from the farmer but a small branch which had blown off a nearby tree; the farmer was round a curve, out of sight, still chivvying some of his sheep off the track and back onto his property. The signalman, now believing that both the up and down lines were clear, pulled off the up signal, noting in his diary as the up express with crewmen Driver Bolton and Fireman Harding hurried past. They had just disappeared round the bend to the south when the signalman heard the urgent squeal of brakes and the sounds of crashing.

"But I heard him knock on my window!" the horrified signalman shouted in desperation to himself as he pulled the up and down signals to 'danger' once more, before rushing outside to see exactly what had happened. As he rounded the bend, he came across a scene of devastation: the engine, tender and the first coach had come off the rails and tipped over on their sides; the left-hand coach side had been forced inwards along half its length. The following three coaches had derailed but were still upright and the remainder of the train appeared to be undamaged. Passengers were clambering out of coach doors and broken windows; a number of injured were already being tended to by those who were only shaken, and a few were wandering about, dazed. The signalman heard the bell of a distant horse-drawn ambulance approaching and a number of local farm labourers were also at the scene, helping where they could.

The front of the prone locomotive was covered in what was obviously blood and the carcasses of several sheep were scattered around it. Driver Bolton had sustained a broken arm and his fireman was badly scalded, but both were alive. The signalman could see, however, at least four corpses of passengers who must have been in compartments of the first coach. They were being laid out carefully by the ambulancemen while the first railway police were arriving. The signalman searched for the farmer who had owned the sheep; he wanted an explanation of why the man had not called out after rounding up his sheep and knocking on the signal box window.

"A sheep farmer?" asked one of the ambulancemen. "We think there was a sheep man among the dead sheep; we put 'im next to the three dead passengers, but ye'll get nowt from 'im, mate; 'e's got no 'ead."

At the later investigation, the signalman was found to have been negligent in not checking that the sheep were off the track and he was demoted to porter status. Yet no further action was taken because, although his claim of a knock on his window could not be confirmed, the glass had a small crack in it, and a section of a branch was found on the ground directly below.

Driver Bolton, with his arm in a splint and sling, saw his fireman being looked after by the side of the track and went over to talk to him. Fireman Harding was lying on a stretcher with much of his torso bound up. He glanced up as his driver came over.

"I'm not too bad, Matt," he said, "but you've got to feel sorry for that pretty girl; by the time she gets to London the prince might have found a new one!"

7 - The Race to the North (April 1895)

The town of Aberdeen had become the target of two groups of railway companies: the London & North Western in company with the Caledonian ran their trains via Carlisle, Stirling and Perth; the Great Northern with the North Eastern and the North British ran via York, Newcastle and Edinburgh. There was strong rivalry between the western and eastern groups, with both striving to provide the faster service to Aberdeen. The competition was spiced up by the need for both groups to use the same tracks from Kinnaber Junction into the city, and when both services were scheduled to arrive at the same time there was deep public interest regarding which company reached Aberdeen first. It was usually the east coast combination.

One sunny evening at London's King's Cross station, on the Great Northern Railway, the large 4-2-2 designed by Patrick Stirling backed onto its Aberdeen train for its run to York, where it would be taken over by a North Eastern engine. The Stirling Single, as it was known, had a fine reputation for both speed and strength, and Driver Reginald Hancock told his fireman that they were going to deliver their train on time at York, come what may. He privately decided that arriving a few minutes early would do no harm and would give the waiting North Eastern engine something of a head start as well. The two companies, working together with the North British, were normally ahead of their western competitors and Reg intended to hammer this fact home. At precisely 8.00pm on the platform, the guard showed his flag and Driver Hancock released the brake, and manipulated the regulator, to take his train out of the station and on up the steep bank, out of the terminus and up to the Copenhagen tunnel.

Taking heavy expresses out of King's Cross was one of the hardest duties of the GNR and express drivers were generally relieved when they reached the summit of the climb with no loss of time. But Reg Hancock knew what his engine could do and by the time they were passing Potters Bar, they were already a minute ahead of the booked timing.

Approaching Doncaster, now three minutes ahead of time, however, they found the signals against them.

"What the hell are they playing at?" Driver Hancock's anger showed in his face as he slowed the train down. "They know we're supposed to get precedence over everything else!"

They were held at the platform as a platform inspector came to explain: "Sorry about this, driver, an axle broke in the station pilot, and we have to get it towed away. You should be off again in a couple of minutes."

In fact, it was nine minutes before they could get away again, with Reg Hancock fuming at having lost the minutes he had striven so hard to win. Between Doncaster and York, he managed to claw back five of them and they arrived in York only two minutes down.

But the North Eastern engine was not waiting ready to take over; it came slowly into view, backing down onto the train which, consequently, left 11 minutes behind time. The engine, a Worsdell-designed 4-4-0 noted for its strength and reliability, gave its crew no problems, although its fireman glanced anxiously at Jamie Nairn, the driver, who appeared to be taking things rather too easily for the express.

"Dinna fash yersel' laddie," said the latter with a smile on his face, "Ah know what ah'm aboot!"

He did; as they ran northwards, it was clear that their speed was steadily increasing and, on observing the station clock at Newcastle where they stopped briefly, they were now only three minutes down. Passing Berwick, they were right on time and Driver Nairn was able to accelerate the train further so that they finally stopped in Edinburgh's Waverly station with two minutes in hand. The North British locomotive coupled on quickly and the train was once more away with no time wasted.

Driver Jenkins was an Englishmen with a penchant for quoting poetry from time to time for the 'edification of his unlearned colleagues', as he expressed it; he had been a student at Edinburgh University until he had decided that academia was not for him. He had joined the NBR as an older cleaner, and with his quick intelligence had rapidly moved up the scale. He had now been driving for seven years.

As they rounded the curve to cross the new Tay bridge, Driver Jenkins glanced at the stumps of the earlier bridge, which had been shattered by a savage storm some few years earlier. The whole train on the bridge at the time had disappeared, with a total loss of passengers and crew, although the locomotive had later been recovered, repaired, and was now running again.

"Tand, tand ist das Gebilde von Menschenhand-" he muttered.

"Whit the hell? Are ye havers, man?"

"Do not show your ignorance, Don; the line is from a famous German poem by Theodor Fontane called *The Tay Bridge*, in which, like Mr Shakespeare's Macbeth, he portrays the disaster as caused by witches."

"Aye, but I still didna understand whit yer said!"

"'Flimsy are the works of man.' It's a great poem. You should read it one day."

"I think I might wait until we're off the bridge."

Driver Jenkins chuckled as they raced over the bridge and soon they were well on their way to Kinnaber Junction.

At eight o'clock on the same evening at Euston station, the LNWR enginemen of the Aberdeen train saw the guard's flag wave and set to work to haul the train up the steep Camden Bank.

"Get ready to bend your back a bit, Jeff," said Driver James Hepplethwaite, "we're non-stop to Crewe and then again non-stop to Carlisle. I want to try and reach Carlisle ten minutes ahead of time if we can. Those East Coast coves have beaten our time so often that they reckon it's their right. Today we're going to surprise 'em."

The enginemen had been very careful in preparing their 2-4-0 'Jumbo' Precedent class express locomotive and they had bribed the Camden shedmaster to ensure they had a supply of top quality coal; they told him they were going to try and get the Night Scotch Express to Aberdeen before their east coast rivals, in spite of the fact that their route to Aberdeen was seventeen miles longer, with two ranges of hills to contend with. Driver Hepplethwaite was annoyed that the North British normally got there well ahead of them.

Once they were up and away past the steep Camden bank, they were able to put on some speed and were passing Watford, then Tring, at well over 70 miles per hour. If they could keep this up as far as Crewe they would be very well-placed to beat their rivals.

On their approach to Crewe, they were racing down Madeley Bank at close to 70, but had to slow down for the stop at the station. Here they were able to enjoy a quick brew and a sandwich while the porters chivvied the passengers quickly on and off the train. They got away seven minutes early but both crewmen knew that the hard part was still to come, through Tebay and over Shap. Beattock in Scotland was another tricky problem but that was for the Caley men to tackle.

The men were still both in good spirits speeding through Wigan, where the station clock showed that they had gained another two minutes on their schedule. It was almost as if their engine knew what they were about and was determined to do its best; it was performing faultlessly. This, it turned out, was very fortunate, as they had to brake sharply when the bright moonglow showed three cows on the line ahead of them. The cowman heard the train and was barely able to drive his cows off the tracks before the train hurtled past him.

The sudden braking lost them three of their precious minutes and both men were swearing as they hurried through Preston. They regained another minute through Lancaster and by Carnforth another had been won. But now they were into the hills and Driver Hepplethwaite said, "Let's have the shovel for a bit, Jeff; I'll spell you as far as Penrith. Keep your eyes peeled for anything else that might give us a problem."

Fireman Jeff Hawkins handed over the shovel with a sigh of relief. "Ta, Jim, I could do with a break." He had fired most of the way from Euston, apart from a ten-minute breather through Stafford, when his driver had taken the shovel.

The short respite over Shap allowed Fireman Hawkins to get his breath back and he took over the firing again with renewed vigour, with the result that they pulled into Carlisle with fourteen minutes in hand.

Ready and waiting at Carlisle was one of the Caledonian's Drummond 4-4-0s, and the engine changeover took place quickly and efficiently. The train left Carlisle with another minute gained.

The Caledonian men had been informed as to the ambitions of their LNWR colleagues and had nodded enthusiastically; they too were unhappy at the constant boasting by the east coast companies that they provided the faster service, particularly as the claim was supported by all the evidence so far. The Drummond 4-4-0s were not noted for any great flights of speed but they were strong engines. Under a good crew – and Driver Willie Fraser and Fireman Patrick McNab were one of the Caley's best – they could put up a performance over the hills which no other Scottish locomotive could match.

The crew's pleasure at having so many minutes in hand after climbing over Beattock was seriously dampened at Carstairs, where a track gang had occupation of the way, to replace a broken point blade. This cost the journey time almost eight minutes and the language of Fireman McNab was suggestive of a stint in the navy in his youth.

Driver Fraser, however, was clearly confident that the eight minutes could be regained. Even he was anxious at Stirling, though; the coach of a local train had derailed on the station throat. Here they lost another five minutes while waiting held up by signals for the station staff to re-rail the coach. Finally, they were signalled through and were able to proceed, albeit at slow speed while gangers checked the trackwork.

With the delays, they had lost thirteen of their fourteen acquired minutes but they still had one in hand.

"It's nae enough, Patrick," said Willie Fraser to his mate, "we'll have tae pick up a few more if we're tae beat the North British crew." Both men concentrated hard and tried to extract all they could out of their locomotive with the result that they reached Kinnaber Junction, where the two routes merged, with no sign of their rivals. The bobby at the signal box gave them a clear run the last few miles of single track to Aberdeen, where they arrived at 6.43am.

Both crewmen on the North British train stared anxiously left at the converging Caledonian tracks at Kinnaber Junction. They knew that if the Caley train was in sight, the Caley bobby in the signal box would hold them and let his own train through, but there was no sign of it and they breathed a sigh of relief as they were powered through to Aberdeen.

"We've done it again, Don. They've missed the bus once more!" Driver Jenkins smiled at his fireman as they slowed down and drew into Aberdeen at 7.06am.

His smile turned to a look of shock as he saw the LNWR coaches stabled in a nearby siding. The Caley driver, his face split into a wide grin, strolled across the platform to their cab; "An' whit kept ye today, lads? Ye couldna get the brakes off yer engine, mebbe? We've bin here mor'n 20 minutes already!"

8 – The Foreign Influence (March 1898)

Mrs Eliza Jenkins marched into the boardroom at Euston, with her broom and duster; there was to be a meeting there at ten o'clock and she wanted to make sure that all the five seats she had been told to prepare were well cleaned. The boardroom reflected the splendour of what was claimed to be the largest private company in the world. But today's meeting was not a full board meeting; the company chairman was meeting with only four senior officials, to discuss a matter which had been on his mind for several weeks.

Eliza gave the last chair a quick flick of her duster as the chairman walked in. The wall clock showed half-past nine. She paled, curtseyed briefly, and hurried out. As she departed, another man appeared, standing aside to let her out as he approached the room.

"Thank you, Mr Barcham, I just wanted a quick word with you before I meet with the financial officers of the company." The chairman indicated a chair and John Barcham sat down carefully, wondering what on earth the chairman wanted with him; a junior electrical engineer with only five years of service with the LNWR.

"You've been with us for five years-"

"Yessir."

"-and in that time you have sent in three reports with suggestions as to how to modify some of our arrangements."

"Er- yessir."

"My chief electrical engineer tells me your suggestions have all been implemented and they have saved the company many thousands of pounds."

John Barcham was startled; he knew that his ideas had worked but had no idea that serious financial gains had been made thereby.

"Besides your obvious technical skills, you have demonstrated a great insight into the workings of complex electrical systems, and an admirable ability to give practical advice. You have very sound judgement for a man of – er, what is it - twenty-seven years of age."

"Sir."

"I am taking you off your regular work because I have another job for you. You are not married, are you?"

"No, sir."

"Good, because you will find yourself frequently out of London.

You will be given a small office here and the assistance of a typist whenever you need one. I want you to spend time around the country, investigating the feasibility of electric traction of trains. This will probably also involve a stay on the Continent as well. I am aware that the Brighton Line, the Midland and the Lanky are looking into electric trains for their suburban systems, and some of the smaller London companies are also planning electric traction for their underground systems. And finally – and this is strictly between ourselves - you are not to mention any details of your findings to anyone but me; is that clear?"

"Yessir!"

Frederick Barcham enjoyed the first few years of his new job in England, spending time talking to colleagues at other railway systems, but soon after found himself lodging with a family in Berlin. His stay in Germany was about to provide him with three surprises.

The first surprise was an invitation from the Prussian military railway to observe a run in their experimental railcar at Marienfelde, a suburb of Berlin. The system looked to him to be rather unwieldy; there were three overhead cables set at differing heights and an unusually clumsy-looking set of pantographs to pick up the three-phase electrical current. Inside the railcar there was a speedometer for the observers to follow progress. This railcar had already proved that it could travel at well over 100 miles an hour. Frederick was not to know that a Great Western locomotive would soon manage this with its train (although the GWR refused to admit to this until almost 20 years later.) He had heard that the Americans had a similar claim, but there was no convincing evidence produced. The German military, however, had proof that they had achieved it.

Sitting in the railcar in October 1903, the ride was quite smooth and the acceleration unbelievably rapid. As the run continued, even the stolid Prussian engineers were becoming excited. Murmurs of amazement could be heard as the speedometer needle rose.

"We had trouble with the overhead cables, Mr Barcham," one of the officials told Frederick, "they were swaying, so we had to move the posts closer together. Then the track needed to be realigned for the high speeds we were anticipat-?"

"Look at that!" an official shouted, interrupting him, "we're over 170kph!"

Two more officials crowded round the speedometer. "Unbelievable!" called one.

"It's still increasing; we're over 190!" the excitement mounted but the exclamations died down as the men watched in growing suspense. "Over 200!"

Then the driver began to slow down; they were fast approaching the terminus at Zossen.

The Prussian authorities were understandably proud of their success and Frederick too was pleased, but for a rather different reason; he was convinced that the LNWR could use electric traction for a suburban network but felt that the three-pole overhead collection was unsuitable. He recommended instead that a ground-level system would be cheaper and more practical.

Frederick's second surprise concerned the family he was staying with. They had a charming young daughter. He had never given much thought to females, and they had not featured in his leisure activities, so the pleasurable intrusion Elke Brettschneider had on his daily thoughts was totally unexpected. When she offered to take him to her choir practice, he immediately accepted; he had never been remotely interested in singing, but the idea of accompanying a very attractive young lady was something he was quite prepared to do. However, Frederick's course of true love was hardly smooth. Elke's regular young man was an army captain who took a very dim view of her friendship with an Englishman, and when she also accompanied Frederick to the theatre, the officer was outraged.

Frederick's third surprise (although shock might be a better term) occurred when the young captain came to see him.

"I forbid you to escort Fräulein Brettschneider, Herr Barcham!" he demanded.

"Surely, Herr Hauptmann Kranz, it is for Fräulein Brettschneider to decide whom she accompanies."

"She is an innocent and impressionable female, Herr Barcham, and must be guided by those of more experience. Tell me, do you English fence?"

"Why yes, we do," replied Frederick, recalling that he had enjoyed his fencing lessons at university.

"Then I challenge you to a duel!"

Frederick was stunned at first: *a duel!* Then he nodded; "I agree! Foils, sabres or épées?"

"We only use sabres. Tomorrow, then, at the University in the Fencing Club?"

"I will be there, Herr Hauptmann, at ten o'clock in the morning."

Arriving at the university, Frederick found that several students were waiting for the spectacle of the bout, and the equipment was set out on a bench for him. He picked it up, wondering at it: a heavy leather jacket, thick gloves and goggles? Why such thick gloves? And why goggles? What about your forehead, your chin, or even your ears?

The Prussian officer walked in, greeted him curtly, proceeded to don the clothing, and then walked over to Frederick and helped him put his on. "Quite different from what we use in England," commented Frederick.

"So?"

Another student walked over to the two men and presented the hilts of the two sabres over his arm, for the combatants to choose from. Frederick drew one sword from the proffered pair and examined his in horror: it had no button, it had a wicked curve, and was razor-sharp; this was a lethal weapon!

He stared at his opponent. "We could seriously injure ourselves with these!"

Hauptmann Krantz looked surprised. "Of course; this is how we test our courage, Herr Barcham!"

Frederick realised why he had seen several students with facial cuts, and his blood ran cold. But before he could protest, he heard the *"En garde!"* He whipped up his sabre just in time to protect his face from a slash to his left cheek. By fighting desperately, he managed to keep himself unblooded for five minutes, before a door burst open and Elke Brettschneider hurried in. "Stop this instant!" she cried angrily. Both men withdrew and lowered their sabres.

"Hauptmann Kranz!" she said angrily, "This is cowardly!"

"Cowardly?" Kranz was astounded. "How so?"

"The English do not duel with open blades."

The Prussian removed his goggles and stared at Frederick in disbelief. "This is true?"

"Yes; we fight with buttons on our swords, and we do not aim to spill blood."

The captain paused, then spoke in obvious embarrassment: "Herr Barcham, I had no idea; I most sincerely apologise. Nevertheless," he added thoughtfully, "you fought very well." He bowed to Elke. "I bid you good day, Fräulein Brettschneider. I will not trouble you further."

With this complication seemingly over, and with Elke Brettscheider's ardent co-operation, Frederick pursued his extra-mural interest to a highly satisfactory conclusion and the pair were married in Berlin a year later.

At his subsequent meeting in London, the Chairman greeted him in a jovial manner: "Well, you'll be pleased to know that we are going to act on your recommendation and apply to Parliament for permission to electrify some of our London suburban system. It will be a while before the politics are all sorted, but we are hopeful, and," added the chairman with a wink, "I hear you've brought back a souvenir from Germany in addition to your technical contribution!"

"Yes indeed, Sir. And my wife will be pleased if we need to visit Berlin again as she will be able to see her family once more."

"Of course she will; however," the chairman paused, showing concern, "political relations between ourselves and the Germans are not as good as they might be. You will need to take care in your conduct with government officials there. The Siemens people are very competent, as you know, and very accommodating to deal with, but they may be under some pressure by their government."

Over the next few years, the LNWR's electric traction proposal received parliamentary approval. The electric motors were supplied and tested, and the coaches were built by Metropolitan-Cammell Carriage and Wagon Company in Saltley, Birmingham, and sent to Wolverton Works to be painted by the LNWR. Frederick, with several other dignitaries, boarded the first set of carriages (borrowed from the District Railway as their own sets were not quite ready) leaving Willesden for Earls Court in May 1914, and was delighted at the comfort and smooth running of the train. Public approval was instant; the system began a limited operation and was an immediate success.

But by early 1914 the political scene had been definitely looking darker and there was talk of a possible war; Frederick advised Elke to go over to Berlin and visit her family once more in case war should break out, making it impossible to see them until the hostilities were over. She was at first reluctant to leave the children with their busy father but finally agreed and left for Berlin in early July of the following year. This was unfortunate timing as the threatened war broke out at the end of that month, and Elke was prevented from returning home. However, as she still had a Prussian passport, she was not interned, and was allowed to stay with her elderly parents.

The war created a problem for LNWR management, since the company had arranged for Siemens to supply them with the necessary electric traction equipment. As well as the sudden shortage of men for recruitment to railway service, their new electric service was so successful that more trains were quickly needed but Siemens was no longer in a position to supply them for ongoing production. Frederick was therefore sent on a somewhat hazardous journey through northern France, where heavy fighting was in progress, to Switzerland. In the town of Oerlikon, it was understood, the Swiss might be able to provide suitable motors for further electric cars. The Swiss had also been active in developing electric traction, and Frederick decided that their motors would be satisfactory to supplement the original Siemens motors. He ordered the required number for the LNWR.

While he was in Switzerland, he wrote to his wife in Berlin to ask whether she could travel to Zürich and meet him, and thus return with him to Britain. It appeared that the German authorities had no objection to journeys to Switzerland and a visit to a Swiss relative in Zürich was given approval.

The couple's reunion was celebrated in the peaceful city and they were able to return uneventfully through France, to catch a ferry across the Channel.

9 - The Bully (March 1904)

There was no question that Driver Hepton, a heavily built and powerful man, had an extremely short fuse. He was inclined to throw his weight about, enjoying the effect this had on others. His regular fireman, Johnny Winslowe, had learned this very quickly and was usually keen to see that the bullying applied to him as little as possible. In this he had an ally; his native wit and sharp tongue had blunted Driver Hepton's aggression on many an occasion, and the driver had found that as a general rule it did not pay to push his fireman around without good reason.

Consequently, the two got on rather better than might have been expected, although there was also no question that Fireman Winslowe relished the rare duty when he was not paired with his regular driver.

Early one morning, Fireman Winslowe was busy outside Camden shed, using a wad of cotton waste to clean the cab side of a Watford 0-6-2T tank engine with which they were scheduled, firstly to shuttle a local from Euston to Watford and back that day, then to take a Bletchley train later.

Bill Hepton appeared, looked at his fireman and grunted, "You missed that bit, Johnny." He pointed to a patch near the number plate.

"No, Mr Hepton, I always like to do the edge first before I clean the inside areas."

"A likely story," muttered Johnny's driver sourly as he climbed into the cab.

The fireman gave the cab side a final wipe and followed him in. "Why are you late today? You're not usually late."

The comment was barbed because Johnny knew that Bill Hepton prided himself on his punctuality, but Johnny felt that the criticism of his cleaning ability had been unwarranted and deserved a counter-attack.

Instead of the outburst expected, the driver simply growled, "Bloody women! On my way to work today I was stopped by a crowd of suffering women with banners - bitches wanted to know whether I thought they should have the vote."

"Ah!" nodded Johnny, "Suffragettes?"

"Aye, that's the word," replied Driver Hepton.

"What did you say?"

"What d'you think I said? I told 'em that women should confine themselves to do what God built 'em to do: have kids, bring up children, cook our meals, and take the odd clip on the ear'ole if they misbe'ave."

"I bet that went down well."

"One of the bitches poked me in the stomach with her umbrella, and I told her she was lucky she wasn't my wife," the driver said angrily, "She'd have got a good deal more than a clip round the ear."

"You're not married, are you, Mr Hepton?"

"Of course I'm not! Can't stand women messing with my things and complaining all the time; won't have one in the house."

"Well who cooks your meals?"

"Mrs Hepton, and she's learned not to touch my gear or complain."

"Mrs Hepton sounds like a woman."

"No, she's my mother."

Their Watford tank was in good condition and there were no mechanical problems on the commuter run to Tring and back. But it was clear that there was considerable female interest in the City as the journey to Euston contained more than the usual number of ladies, many of whom were carrying banners. Driver Hepton spent the breaks and much of the driving time explaining to his fireman how women were ruining the country with their unnatural wishes to run matters that rightly belonged to men. Johnny wisely kept his opinion to himself; he wanted an easy shift without any arguments which he knew would irritate his driver. However, his wish not to have his driver annoyed on this shift was to be seriously undermined.

On their return from Tring, they were to take a semi-fast to Bletchley and return with a parcels to Euston. Arriving in Bletchley, they handed over their locomotive to a local crew to take it to the shed for servicing while they waited on the platform for their parcels train to arrive from the north. They were waiting on the main up platform while a local shuttle was due to arrive from Birmingham New Street. Awaiting this arrival as well were several ladies who were discussing the Suffragette Movement with some vigour. Johnny Winslowe, worried that his driver might intervene in the discussion with at least equal enthusiasm, suggested that they move away from the women and buy their tea in the nearby canteen.

"Tea?" Bill Hepton was surprised, "Why pay for tea when we can get it for free in our own cab?"

"Er - it's just that..."

"Nonsense! Our train might come in any minute now and we need to relieve the crew as quickly as we can."

At that moment Driver Hepton heard one of the women claim loudly to her friend that a woman could do most things a man could, and do them better. He immediately turned on the woman and began to argue with her. Johnny tried to distract him but Bill Hepton was in full swing and had the attention of a gathering crowd of indignant females. He found himself surrounded by them, and with a glaring lack of tact pointed out in language unsuited to feminine ears two or three intimate activities which females were anatomically incapable of. Accompanying these remarks with a finger pushed indelicately into one of the ladies, he received an angry cry of protest and a firm nudge from a sharp parasol. This was doubly unfortunate as he was standing at the edge of the platform, and the nudge toppled him over onto the track, along which their parcel train was now slowing down, unnoticed by either Driver Hepton or his fireman.

Spreadeagled on the track, the driver stood up again, ready to give full vent to his wrath when the arriving parcels train, headed by an Experiment class 4-6-0, slowed down almost to a stop, only to knock him off balance once more.

By great good fortune, he was only slightly bruised as the train stopped with a jerk.

Climbing back onto the platform with murder in his eyes, Bill Hepton discovered that the ladies had all merged with the other waiting passengers. He could not see the one who had pushed him and was in any case unable to describe her with any useful accuracy to the police constable who had appeared.

Appealing to his fireman was of little use; Johnny claimed he had not seen who had nudged his driver as a large lady had been standing between them and had obscured his view of the incident. In the meantime, the arriving crewmen, neither of whom had seen Driver Hepton on the track, had climbed down to hand over the cab to them and to discover the reason for the disturbance on the platform.

As the arriving train was already two minutes late, Driver Hepton had no alternative but to climb quickly into the cab with his fireman and try to make up the lost time. Johnny sighed quietly to himself; his colleague was in a savage mood and the return to Euston was going to be a trying experience. At least, Johnny consoled himself, they were taking a parcels train so there were no passengers, female or otherwise, with whom the red-faced driver could fight. Nevertheless, the unfortunate fireman had plenty of shovelling to do as the driver thrashed his engine, pulling great holes in Johnny's carefully tended fire. As soon as he had filled one hole, another appeared. The engine, with its heavy racing parcels train, was riding very roughly and the luckless Johnny had to hold on as well as fire.

At least, Johnny thought, *I won't have to take the blame for any early arrival.*

Early arrivals were considered to be signs of poor driving and were much harder to justify than the far more common late arrivals, which could usually be explained by signalling hold ups or other incidents.

On the approach to Euston, instead of letting the train coast down the long Camden bank, Bill Hepton continued to drive. Their speed over the crossovers at the station throat was such that he had to brake very sharply in the platform, and even then the train hit the buffers with some force, causing considerable hilarity among the porters, who were gathering to assist with unloading the parcels. Their open amusement did nothing to calm Bill Hepton down; he jumped from the cab and strode towards them, intent on giving them a piece of his mind and, possibly, his fist.

This, as it turned out, was a bad mistake. Driver Hepton was not the only furious man on the platform; their guard, who was smaller but had a distinctly no-nonsense air about him, came storming along and vented his own anger at the driver.

"Whit the bluidy hell d'ye mean by steaming in at sich a pace? That was the most dangerous piece of driving I've iver seen!" His Scottish accent was made stronger by his indignation.

Bill grabbed the shorter man by the lapels and thrust his face close in. "What did you say?" he thundered.

The guard did not flinch. "Call yersel' a driver? I've seen cleaners driving better than that. An' tak yer hands off ma jacket!"

Johnny Winslowe, watching the altercation, was hoping he wouldn't be witness to a murder.

For God's sake man, he thought to himself, *back off and apologise to the driver while you've still got a face!*

But Bill Hepton pulled the guard's lapels together with his left hand and drew back his right fist.

"I'm going to punch your lights out!" he roared. "You cheeky little bastard!" But the punch did not materialise; instead, he gasped as the little guard lifted a knee swiftly into his crotch. As the driver's head bent forward in agony, the Scot hit him with his own forehead.

"Be thankful I've on'y given ye a wee Glasgae kiss!" said the guard as Driver Hepton writhed in torment on the platform. He curled up into a foetal position, blood pouring from his face.

The guard turned to Johnny, "He'll be sore fer a couple of days but he'll nae need a doctor. Tell him that next time he wants a fight ter pick someone his ain size!"

"Where on earth did you learn to fight like that?"

"Och, ma basic trainin' was on the streets o' Glasgae as a young fella, but I had whit ye might call 'advanced training' in the war with the Boers in '02." He looked again at the injured man still lying on the ground. "Gie 'im a couple of days and he'll be drivin' once more. But he'll no' be so ready wi' his fist again!"

However, it was only a day later when Driver Hepton turned up for duty once more. Johnny Winslowe sighed; he had been hoping for at least two more days with peaceful shifts.

Bill Hepton was immediately called in to explain the serious damage to a consignment of valuable antiques in the parcels train. The Camden shed foreman was not worried about the cost; insurance would cover that. He was, however, very angry about the danger caused by the reckless driving. He removed Driver Hepton from the top link and placed him back into a lower one, "to sharpen up your driving skills." He also warned the driver that another incident would result in further demotion or even dismissal from the company.

On hearing this welcome news, Johnny was delighted, but his pleasure was somewhat muted when he heard that his regular driver would now be Patrick O'Leary.

Like most of the LNWR enginemen at Camden shed, Johnny liked Patrick, but working with him had its own distinct hazards. The Irishman was a great one for practical jokes...

10 - The Demon Drink (February 1905)

Johnny Winslowe's first four days with his new driver had been worrying. Patrick O'Leary was a far better senior driver than Bill Hepton had been, and furthermore he was much better company; cheerful, helpful and good-natured. On the one hand, it was a pleasure to be firing to a man who was not permanently critical and generally morose; on the other, Johnny had been constantly watchful for anything which might presage a leg-pull of some kind. This had been wearing on his nerves and he suspected that Patrick was waiting for him to relax before trying anything. Johnny continued to be alert to any possibility and on their fifth day together he began to suspect that he was right, as he observed a mischievous smile on Patrick's face. Johnny was instantly on his guard.

Their shift consisted of drawing the up express passenger coaches from the arrival platforms at Euston and shunting them into the carriage sidings for cleaning and readying for their next turn. For this they had been allocated an 0-6-2T 'coal tank', entirely suited to this duty. They had completed the myriad chores on the engine before their shift: the water tanks had been topped up, the motion oiled, brakes checked, and so on. Johnny had built up the fire such that the steam pressure in the boiler was sufficient to allow them to run down the grade to Euston ready to draw the heavy rake of coaches from the up *Irish Mail* which had just arrived, back into the carriage sidings. Johnny eyed the big 4-4-0 express passenger Precursor class locomotive as it passed, wondering how long it would be before he could fire and (the thought was almost too much) actually drive one.

After the mail coaches, they collected and disposed of a Liverpool rake, then a rake from Glasgow which included a number of Caledonian Railway coaches, pausing in the sidings for a morning tea break.

Johnny noted a gleam in Patrick's eye as the latter offered him some extra sugar from a glass jar, claiming it as an 'extra gift from me missus'. Johnny accepted gladly - he had a sweet tooth - but commented that while they were temporarily stationary, Patrick might have a look at the front coupling as it was curiously stiff.

Patrick nodded, "Oi'll do it now before me tea."

"Thanks," said Johnny, "I'll just have a sip and come and show you what I mean."

Patrick climbed down the left-hand steps and Johnny tipped Patrick's tea over the coal in the bunker, refilling the driver's mug with his own drink.

"Seems foine ter me," said Patrick when Johnny joined him in front of the engine, "Where was it stickin'?"

"P'raps your efforts freed it up," suggested Johnny as he lifted it. "You're right, it's a lot easier now. Ta, Mr O'Leary."

Back in the cab, Patrick picked up his mug and took a deep swallow of his tea. Johnny watched quietly. Patrick's eyes widened and his face went red before he put his mug slowly down on the shelf over the fire doors. He stared at his fireman then a huge grin gradually spread over his face, as he tipped his tea into the firebox.

"Ach, yer a crafty little bugger, Johnny Winslowe, so ye are! Oi'll 'ave ter watch meself around ye!"

Johnny grinned, "What was in the tea?"

"Salt," said Patrick as he turned to the regulator to get ready to follow a Wolverhampton express down to the Euston terminus.

"Hey, look at that first coach!" called Johnny as the express passed them; a door at the end was open.

"That's not good!" said Patrick gravely as he saw what Johnny was pointing at, "We'd better warn them when we back on to the train to take the rake to the sidings."

They finished their tea and waited for the points to permit them onto the main line and the signal to indicate that they could follow the express down the bank to Euston. Arriving behind the stationary coaches, Johnny climbed down to couple up while Patrick went to warn the guard of the open door in the first coach.

"Yes," said the guard as he checked his train journal, "I noticed one passenger was missing sometime after we left Tring. The beggar must have fallen out somewhere. We'll have to notify the platform inspector."

As they spoke, the inspector came over to find out why the driver of the coal tank was talking to the guard of the express. When they explained, he thought for a moment then instructed Patrick to get his engine uncoupled once more.

"I want you to drive light engine up as far as Tring and see what you can on either side of the line," he said, "I'll get another engine to take the Wolverhampton coaches away."

Patrick nodded and called Johnny to uncouple again and they both climbed back into the cab and waited for the down platform starter signal to drop and allow them out of the platform. They had to wait a few minutes for the down slow line to be cleared before they could proceed, and then they moved off up the bank, speeding as far as the sidings where Johnny had first seen the open door on the express. After that, they moved more slowly, in order to check on both sides of the tracks in case there was any sign of a passenger having fallen from the train.

Just before Tring, they were held up by a signal check. Johnny was leaning out of the cab looking at the trackside when he noticed a small bush about ten yards from the track. It had what appeared to be a foot sticking out of it. As the signal changed to clear, Patrick began to lift the regulator but Johnny called out.

"Hang on a mo, Mr O'Leary; we may have found the missing passenger."

The driver applied the brake and stopped the engine with a slight jerk then moved over to see what his fireman was staring at.

"Ye could be roight, Johnny me bhoy. Nip down an' have a close look."

Johnny climbed down from the cab and went over to the bush, lifted a couple of branches, and peered under.

"Yep, I think it's him," he called back, "but I'm pretty sure he's a goner. It looks like his neck's broken."

Patrick joined him and agreed. "You stay here an' keep watch, an' Oi'll drive on to Tring and inform the stationmaster."

It was only half a mile to Tring station, and the coal tank was soon back with the stationmaster and a brace of policemen in the cab, one of them a sergeant. The policemen climbed down and hauled the body out of the bush.

"Aye, he's a goner alright," commented the sergeant, "His neck's at an impossible angle, and..." he looked again, "I think he's been murdered!"

"Murdered?" queried the constable in surprise, "Why'd you say that, Sarge?"

"Here," the sergeant turned the body onto its front. "There's what might be a stab wound in his back!"

He turned to the stationmaster, "Would the guard have a record of any of the passengers, sir?"

The stationmaster shook his head, "Not normally, no. He just keeps the train journal to record the number of passengers boarding and alighting at each stop."

"Well, I'll have to inform my inspector and we'll probably have detectives up here shortly; they'll want to look around for clues. My constable can stay here with the body and perhaps I can come back with you to the station?"

"Yes, of course. Will you need the engine crew here? They're still on duty."

"No, sir, I don't think so. The detectives will want to interview them but they can do that at Euston."

The stationmaster nodded. "Thank you."

The sergeant climbed back into the cab and Patrick drove them back to Tring station, leaving the constable to guard the body. Patrick and Johnny returned to Euston to report to the platform inspector for further orders and were told to continue with their duty of drawing coaches back from the arriving expresses into the sidings.

At the end of their shift they both had to speak to a detective, who wrote down their replies in his notebook, but there wasn't much they could tell him that he didn't know already.

"It's all corroboration," he explained, "If different witnesses say the same thing, we can assume it's likely to be correct. Very helpful, that is."

"Different witnesses?" queried Patrick. "What other witnesses?"

"A lady on a bridge over the railway saw something."

"What did she see?"

The detective shook his head and smiled, "Ah, now that's police business. Can't tell you that!"

The following day they were back on a similar duty to that of the day before, except they were taking coaches from the sidings down to the departure platforms at Euston, ready for the down expresses. As Johnny coupled on the same Wolverhampton rake of the previous day's drama, he noticed a brown lanyard jammed in a cleft near the corridor connection. He called to his driver.

"Mr O'Leary, come and look at this."

Patrick climbed down to look and stared at the bayonet attached to the lanyard, "Begorrah Johnny, ye're in the wrong job; 'tis the coppers ye should've joined! We'll 'ave to fetch one ter look at this!"

The yardmaster was annoyed at this interruption to the shift and the paperwork which would be involved, but agreed that the police would certainly need to be called in.

The detective arrived once more and was impressed as he took the bayonet and examined it. "This will be a great help to us, this is a military bayonet and there was a small detachment of soldiers on the train. We just need to find one without his bayonet and discover why he lost it."

Two days later, Johnny was again called into the foreman's office; the detective was also there again. "Thanks to you," he smiled, "we've found the man involved in the death of the passenger. It was a soldier on the train. He had an argument with the passenger - both of them had been drinking heavily in the restaurant car of the express, it seemed - and in the course of a fight, somehow they got the door open and the passenger fell out after he had apparently been knifed, presumably by the soldier. The soldier himself is in a bad way, he was slashed across the face by his own bayonet; he's in a military hospital now and will be handed over to us when he has recovered."

"What will happen to him?" asked Johnny.

"That's not for us to say; that will be a matter for the judge and jury. He may hang for murder, but I think that's unlikely; I think he'll get a prison sentence for manslaughter. He might even get off if they find he acted in self-defence. The dead man might have been killed by falling out of the train; the coroner will have to decide that."

"Plenty of toime ter get drunk between Wolverhampton and Tring," commented Patrick, "a Guinness or two is enough fer me at the pub once or twice a week. Me woife and Father Callaghan see to that."

"There's another thing," added Johnny to the detective, "Any drunkenness in the cab means instant dismissal for us; the London and North Western is very strict about that."

The yardmaster nodded, "Last week the shedmaster at Banbury dismissed a senior driver when he found a half-empty bottle of whisky hidden under the coal in the man's tender. Kicked out after 43 years of service, he was."

"But he'll simply have gone to another railway company and got another driving job won't he?" asked the detective.

"Not at all, railway companies don't want other railways' cast-offs. They'd want to know why he left the LNWR and when they found out, they wouldn't even interview him."

"There ye go, Johnny me bhoy," was Patrick's comment, "Me tea moight not taste the best, but at least it won't get ye the sack!"

11 - The Apprentice (August 1905)

It was just on five o'clock when there was a knock at the door of the Thurston farm, not far from Beeston Castle in central Cheshire. John Thurston saw a small, well-dressed man standing looking at him.

"Mr Thurston?" enquired the man.

"Yes, that's me; who are you and what do you want?" John had been about to have his tea and didn't relish this interruption.

The visitor removed his hat, "My name is Campling, and I teach your son, Paul. I wonder if I might have a few words with you?"

"Ah, then I'm so glad you came, Mr Campling. Please come in," replied John, opening the door wide. He led his visitor into a tidy front room. "I was hoping to get time to come and see you about Paul's report; it's not what we were hoping for."

"No, it doesn't give an indication of his real potential. His work is often hampered by a lack of attention, and I..."

"If he's lazy, there's a simple solution," John Thurston touched his belt.

"No, no," replied Campling hurriedly, "Nothing like that. I am sure he's just tired."

"Ah, well that's possible. My farm labourer has been ill for a few weeks and Paul has to help out; he's up at five to look after the milking and feed the hens before he goes to school."

"Does he enjoy farm work?"

John hesitated then admitted, "Not really; he's a good lad, so he does it, but his heart's not in it."

Mr Campling opened his briefcase and removed a sheaf of papers.

"I'd like to show you something," he said, spreading the papers out on a side table. "A couple of weeks ago I took my class around Crewe Works; my brother is a fitter there. Later I gave the boys some paper and told them to draw the thing that most interested them."

He laid out a dozen drawings one by one on the table. Most were of engines and were of the standard one would expect from young teenage boys. One of the sketches, however, was an excellent coloured drawing of a coach.

"You did one as well?" asked John, "To show them how to draw?"

"No, Mr Thurston, I did not draw one. That is your son's."

John Thurston stared at the drawing in disbelief. "Paul did that?"

"Indeed he did. And that was without taking any notes; we were in the paint shop for no more than ten minutes."

"It's good, I must say."

"There's more to it than you might think, Mr Thurston. Look at the detail around the windows. The LNWR has complex colours for its coaches. It's not merely the 'dark plum and spilt milk' as people say; the beading has a yellow line round it with very fine white borders, and the window frames are mahogany. The scheme is detailed and complicated, and Paul has got it just right. He was working quickly and with enthusiasm. I showed this picture to the foreman of the paint shop. He said the next apprentice intake is in three weeks' time, and if Paul wanted to apply and did work like this again he would be certain to be accepted."

"You mean work for the railway?"

"It's something you might consider for him."

"Let me call his Ma for a moment - Emily! Can you come here for a minute?"

Mrs Thurston was a lady in her late 30s, with an air of competence about her. She listened as her husband explained the situation, paused for a moment then said, "We will talk to Paul."

This, Campling understood, was not a suggestion, it was a directive.

"If he agrees," Emily Thurston continued, "he'll apply. And thank you, Mr Campling, for taking the trouble over our son."

With that, she left the room. *A formidable woman!* thought Campling to himself.

Some three weeks later, Paul was sitting in a room at Crewe Works among the two dozen other applicants, all of them sitting with their heads bowed, writing the answers to a variety of questions on an exam paper. A preliminary medical exam had been conducted in the morning, and those deemed fit for railway service were now sitting the written exam. Paul was startled to see a large ink blot suddenly appear on his paper; he looked up to see the next boy grinning at him. The boy flicked another blob of ink over but Paul swiftly put his hand over his paper and the ink fell on his skin. As the boy tried to flick a third blob over, he yelped in sudden pain as his ear was firmly grasped and he was hauled out of his seat. The boy's paper was picked up by the supervisor, who tore it up and dropped it into a rubbish bin.

"The LNWR doesn't need idiots, off you go," he said shortly before turning to Paul, "Don't worry about the blot on your paper, I saw how it got there."

After another hour, the supervisor called out, "Make sure you have your names on your papers, then put your pens down. Your parents will receive a letter with your results in a week's time."

Fifteen young lads were sitting once more in the same room a fortnight later, listening to the same supervisor noting down their details. They had already been interviewed and were in several groups. One group of eight were issued with cleaner's equipment and clothing. Three more were to be railway clerks. Two were being posted to signalling, and Paul and another lad – Alan - were to be sent to the paint shop.

"You lads will have to put up with a certain amount of teasing from the older apprentices, but keep your noses clean and obey the instructions of your charge-hands and the London and North Western Railway will look after you," advised the supervisor.

The paint shop smelt so strongly that Paul and Alan almost gagged as they entered. At one end a short horsebox had just been refurbished with replacement wood panels and was waiting to be repainted; next to it a coach was engaging the attention of a number of men who were painting the upper cream panels, while another painter was applying the yellow edging to the upper beading. An apprentice was painting the lower panels of a luggage van, under the close watch of a senior painter. Two other apprentices were mixing large tins of paint to reach the consistency and tint required by the watchful charge-hand who saw the two boys enter and came over.

"Albert Palfrey at your service, lads," he began, "You'll be the two new apprentices we were expecting."

"Yes sir," both replied.

"Well, the North Western expects good, hard work from its trainees on a month's probation, and if it gets it, you'll be employed on a more permanent basis."

The two boys nodded keenly, eager to show the LNWR that it could rely on them to do their best.

After a couple of months, both boys had begun to settle into the job; they had learned how to mix paints to the required shade for the particular job in hand and had begun, under the supervision of charge-hand Palfrey, to paint goods wagons.

Paul always made sure to arrive at work early so that he could spend half an hour at the station watching the trains; he was fascinated by the variety of colours that could be seen. In many companies, the engine crews were responsible for the external appearance of their engines, and could be fined if the locomotive's appearance did not come up to scratch. As a result, in major junctions like Crewe or Carlisle, into which several companies ran their stock, the trains displayed a remarkable range of colours.

In Crewe could be seen the Midland and the North Stafford stock with their crimson red coaches, as well as the Great Western with their Brunswick green engines and new colour scheme of red-brown coaches. Occasionally there were through coaches from the south, such as the dark maroon SECR and the LSWR which were dark brown and salmon pink. From Manchester and Liverpool came the Lancashire and Yorkshire stock with their dark and light brown. Caledonian coaches, purple-brown with white upper panels, from the Anglo-Scottish expresses appeared on a daily basis. Paul loved to try and catch the various hues by sketching on his pad in his spare time, whilst the other boys played football in their tea breaks.

One day Mr Palfrey had taken all the apprentices into a smaller paint shop to explain the finer points of mixing paints, when he was called away for a few minutes.

One of the older apprentices, Alec Collier, put his brush down. "Time fer a quick drag," he grinned, pulling out and lighting a cigarette then sitting down next to the coach he was working on.

He didn't get much of a chance to relax, however; another apprentice by the door hissed out to him, "Put the fag out, you daft sod! He's coming back!"

Alec swore, dropping his butt. It fell into some paint he had spilt and immediately started a small fire.

"Gawdalmighty!" he cursed, staring at the flames. Grabbing a pot of tea, he poured it onto the fire, but it had little effect.

Paul ran over, seized a bucket of sand and tipped it on the fire, putting out the flames. As Mr Palfrey returned, he saw the mess and stared around grimly.

"Who was it?" he asked quietly, but got no reply. "I see. Then I'll see each of you separately in my office, starting now."

He summoned the first boy to follow him in.

Half an hour later, Albert Palfrey called the group together in the paint shop.

"This is a very serious matter. Burning paint could have done a great deal of damage and even ended up with fatalities here." He paused. "There is another matter; the works manager tells me we don't need so many apprentices, so two of you will be leaving us. Collier and Thurston, into my office please, now."

The other boys were shocked into silence. A few moments later,

Alec Collier came out, collected his belongings and left without a word. There was no sign of Paul. Mr Palfrey came back shortly afterwards and announced that Alec Collier had been sacked, then with a gleam in his eye, he added that Paul Thurston would not be slapping paint on rolling stock any more either.

"But why, sir?" asked one of the apprentices, horrified.

"Paul has been transferred," said Mr Palfrey.

"But he put the fire out!" said the apprentice. "We all saw him!"

"Oh, I know that," Albert produced one of his very rare smiles. "He has not been punished. Quite the reverse, in fact. He has shown a most unusual talent for colours and has been transferred to the North Western's headquarters at Euston. The company needs a competent, specialist railway artist to supplement its black and white photography and record the details in colour. We believe young Thurston is just the man for the job."

12 - The Bank Robber (September 1906)

The manager of the Williams Deacons bank in Audenshaw, a suburb of Manchester, was puzzled by his client; the man was smartly dressed as a gentleman, with a well-fitting suit, polished shoes and a top hat, but he had the unmistakable accent of a workman. Yet the manager could find no fault at all with the written references presented; they were impeccable. He therefore could see no reason not to agree to the loan of two thousand pounds. The money had been brought by a teller and was now inside the client's portmanteau, from which without any warning the man produced a pistol, chain and a padlock. Threatening the manager with the gun, he proceeded to chain him to his chair and then opened the door of the office and slipped out.

He menaced the four shocked tellers with his pistol and snapped, "Dahn on the floor, all o' yer! I've got yer boss chained up an' I want no trouble. Now, where's yer bog? I 'ave ter go for a piss, an' if any o' yer's not on the floor when I come out, I'll shoot yer boss!"

One of the tellers on the floor pointed silently to a small door and the man went in. Once inside, he rapidly took off his outer clothes and put on a dirty jacket and trousers from his bag. He left the abandoned clothes on the floor and dropped the padlock down the lavatory before pulling the chain and opening the small high window. Climbing out, he threw his bag onto the pavement and lowered himself down, then, putting a cloth cap on his head, he took up his bag and strolled round the corner into the main road where he caught a passing tram heading for London Road station in Manchester.

The express trundled off the main North Wales tracks, crossed the main station throat and drew up slowly into the far left platform of Crewe station.

"Crewe, this is Crewe," could be heard over the murmurings of the crowd as the train stopped with a squeal of brakes and then, "Next stop Stafford, then Rugby and London Euston." The porter repeated himself a few moments later as the passengers jostled to board the train with their luggage and find seats for themselves.

In the cab of the locomotive, an express 4-4-0 of the Precursor class, Driver Henry Burkinshaw commented, "I hear the king is not too fit, Freddy; they say he's going downhill."

Freddy Pugh, the fireman, paused in placing another shovelful of coal into the locomotive's firebox, "Yeah, I 'eard summat about that too, and the ol' queen not that long in 'er box neither."

Freddie turned back to the tender to pick up some more coal. After glancing in the firebox to check that all was as it should be, he noticed that the porters were still busy loading parcels into the luggage van at the rear of the train.

"Could be 'ere fer a while yet, Mr Burkinshaw," he said, "There's a lot to be loaded."

"I'll have a quick look round the engine, then," said the driver, climbing down onto the platform and walking to the front of the locomotive. They had picked up the engine from Chester LNWR shed, and as it had just been cleaned that day, it shone in its gleaming blackberry gloss paint with the red, grey and cream lining. Henry climbed up onto the footplate to give the brass plate bearing the name *Sirocco* a quick shine with a cloth. The coaches were equally clean and were a dark plum below the waist and the colour of skim milk above. The smart appearance of the train was one of the reasons why the LNWR called itself 'The Premier Line' and few could disagree. The company was proud of its colour scheme and tried hard, as did many of the other railway companies in the kingdom at that time, to maintain high standards of cleanliness in their stock. Indeed, in these years before the First World War, the appearance of the rolling stock of Britain's railways had reached a pinnacle never again achieved in the 20th century.

"We've got the starter, Mr Burkinshaw!" called the fireman from the cab and the driver, giving the red nameplate with its gold lettering a final rub, climbed back in.

"Right, let's be off then," he said, easing the regulator gently upwards, to the admiring gaze and envious glance of his fireman, as the train began to move off almost imperceptibly. Henry Burkinshaw was a master driver, and many firemen of Chester shed would have liked to be in Freddy Pugh's shoes, learning from one of the best.

At Stafford, as they heard the guard's whistle for the off, Freddy looked back down the train and noticed a man running across the footbridge and down the steps. The train began to move slowly as Henry lifted the regulator and the man caught up with the last coach, opened a door, threw in the bag he was carrying, then jumped, slamming the door behind him.

"Lucky fella!" commented Freddy as he took hold of his shovel.

"Who?" asked Henry, watching the road ahead through the cab's spectacle plate.

"Oh, some bloke wot ran along the platform an' just caught the last coach."

"Huh," Henry wasn't interested. He had found a speck of coal dust on the spectacle plate and was cleaning it off.

The engine was humming along nicely and all was well as they raced through Rugeley and slowed down for the run through the platform at Lichfield, where waiting passengers grabbed hold of their hats to prevent the express from blowing them off as it swept through. Henry lifted the regulator again as they had no further stops until Rugby, a good half hour away. Approaching Nuneaton, however, he muttered a quiet curse, eased the regulator, and the train began to slow.

Freddy stopped shovelling and looked up at his driver. "What's up?"

"We've got the distant against us," grumbled Henry, "Don't know why. We should be given a clear run through here to Rugby; must be something slow ahead of us."

A short while later, Freddy looked out of the right-hand spectacle plate and said, "Hey! we've got the home against us too!! We'll 'ave to stop!"

"What the hell are they playing at?" Henry was angry, "Must be something heavy!"

They slowed and stopped at the signal in a cutting; along the train, heads were poking out of the windows to see what the hold-up was. A lorry pulled up and stopped on a bridge and, as they waited, a dozen policemen clambered out then scrambled down the bank, while three more could be seen running to the tracks from the other side. They were all heading for the rear carriage of the train. A door opened and a man jumped out, carrying a bag. He paused and took out a pistol from his pocket, firing at the police who all ducked; all except for one, who staggered and fell. The fugitive turned and ran swiftly alongside the train, well ahead of the pursuing police.

Freddy picked up his shovel and threw it at the running man as he passed the engine. The blade hit the man's leg, causing him to lurch and fall over.

"Watch yourself, Freddy, he's armed!" called Henry as his fireman dropped from the cab to pick up his shovel.

"Yer've cut me leg, yer bastard!" groaned the fallen man, aiming his pistol at Freddy and firing at point blank range. But Freddy had picked up his shovel with the blade in front of him; the bullet hit the blade and sang harmlessly away. Freddy swung his shovel again and knocked the pistol out of the man's hand.

"Well done, lad!" came a shout from the leading policeman, as he reached the pair. He seized the groaning man, yanked him over on his back, ignoring the yelp of pain, and snapped a pair of handcuffs on him before turning him savagely back on his front.

"Two thousand quid, eh? Was it worth the ten years you'll get?" He paused then added, "Or if my mate dies, you'll swing - and that'll be no great loss!"

Formalities and acquiring the details of the two enginemen took ten more minutes until the train was permitted to continue. Back in the cab, Freddy explained to his driver what the police had told him.

"Apparently he nicked the money from some bank in Manchester but was spotted climbing out of the bog's winder an' catchin' a city-bound tram. The witness told a nearby copper wot 'e'd seen an' 'e told 'is sergeant. The description was sent to the city police stations but the coppers just missed 'im at London Road station, as 'e caught an 'ereford train. They telephoned stations down the line but missed 'im again at Salop where 'e changed an' caught a Great Western train ter Wellington. They caught up with 'im there but 'e again dodged 'em and caught our train to Stafford. They tried to grab 'im quietly at Stafford but didn't know 'e 'ad a gun an' 'e got away again, the slippery bugger. No wonder the coppers 'ad trouble catchin' up with 'im!'

"Then he met Fearsome Freddy Pugh," said Henry with a grin, "I must admit that using your shovel as a shield was a very smart move. Never seen anything like it."

"Err - yeah, well..." Freddy had the grace to look sheepish, "that was an accident; I was actually goin' to belt 'im one on the napper, but 'e shot 'is pistol before I could 'it 'im."

"We won't mention that to the police when they question us in detail - as they will at Euston."

Two days later, back in Chester shed, Freddy's exploit was the talk of the enginemen. "Young bugger'll be so big 'eaded 'e'll not fit into a cab anymore," commented one elderly driver to Henry outside the wall of the coaling plant, "I don't know 'as 'ow you'll stick with 'im, Henry!"

"I'll stick with him for two very good reasons," replied Henry.

"Wot?"

"One: he's not a bad fireman."

"And the other?"

"With him and his shovel in the cab with me, I feel much safer!"

13 - The Two Firemen (May 1907)

Fireman Gerry Marshall stood at the end of Platform Four at Chester General Station, waiting to take over from the Manchester crew on the crack Club train to Llandudno. He sighed when he saw the big 4-6-0 Experiment class engine. There were two problems: the locomotive and the driver.

The Experiment class engines were, in theory, more powerful than their 4-4-0 predecessors but were very hard to fire effectively. The main problem lay in the design of the firebox, which was shallower than that of the Precursor class, thus making it very difficult to throw the coal into the right part of the firebox for it to have the required effect. He much preferred the Precursors, which were far easier to fire.

As for the second problem, Danny Brent was a fine driver, but rather too fond of a jar or two whenever they had a break, and he was inclined to leave his fireman to look after everything on his own.

The run to Llandudno was, however, without incident but Llandudno was a terminus, and as soon as they had pulled in at the buffer stops, Danny turned to Gerry. "Right, you know what to do."

The driver promptly disappeared in the direction of the nearest pub.

On receiving the shunter's nod, Gerry nervously backed the train out of the station and into a carriage siding, uncoupled the engine, drove it onto the turntable, and turned it - ready for its return journey. He then parked it, cleaned the fire and took on water, before having his own wash and sandwiches.

Collecting the coaches for a stopper to Chester, he backed the train into the station and waited for his driver, who arrived with a mere minute to spare before departure time, to Gerry's intense relief.

"You drive, I'll fire," said Danny, who needed to flex his muscles after spending two hours sitting in a pub.

Gerry nodded.

Danny's idea of teamwork was extremely risky, and had this been noticed by a platform inspector, he almost certainly would have been sacked. On the other hand, Gerry welcomed the chance to drive, and Danny did not take over the regulator until Mold Junction a few miles west of Chester.

Back in Crewe North enginemen's cabin, Driver Alan Woking nodded knowingly as a tired Gerry entered. "Danny give you the regulator again, did he?"

"Yes," answered Gerry, "Llandudno to Mold Junction."

Alan shook his head, "One of these days, he'll get the boot if he's not careful. Still, getting you to drive a bit is no bad thing - unlike poor old Bill over there."

They both looked across at Fireman Bill Winter.

"You look knackered, Bill."

Bill Winter shrugged his shoulders as he got up to leave, "Firing to Driver Jones isn't easy."

Alan nodded sympathetically; they all knew that Huw Jones was a hard man. Then the door opened and Driver Jones himself walked in, looking for his fireman. Drivers Jones and Woking loathed each other, and at once the atmosphere in the cabin became tense.

Driver Jones called to his fireman, "Thought I'd find you here loafing. Get off your bum, we've got work to do."

Bill Winter left but as Driver Jones tried to leave, Alan Woking stood in his way. Jones became red in the face and clenched his fists, ready for either defence or attack, whichever was called for.

Alan Woking poked a finger at him. "You're nothing but a lazy tyke, Jones. Your poor bloody fireman does all the work in your cab and you just stand there at the regulator and give the poor bastard instructions. Why don't you ever take the shovel and give him a hand from time to time like the rest of us do?"

"I've done all my shovelling days; that's Winter's job, not mine! That's what he's paid for; why the hell should I do his work for him?"

Bill Winter had been taken ill after a two-week stint on the run from Crewe to Euston and back; the train had been a heavy express and the engine was not in the best condition. Most drivers would have taken pity on the fireman in such circumstances and taken over the firing for a spell, but Jones had kept him at it without a break from Crewe to Euston and back, almost ten hours non-stop firing every day. The drivers standing around nodded in agreement; they all knew from experience what firing such a train was like, and every one of them would have taken a turn on the shovel. The maintenance of LNWR engines was no better or worse than that of other companies, but all engines could provide their crews with problems when it was nearing time for a visit to the repair shop. Jones had now realised that he was not going to be attacked and had lowered his fists, but seeing the distinctly unfriendly faces around him, he turned and walked out of the enginemen's cabin.

Fireman Dennis Braithwaite was a Quaker and a quiet, unassuming man who was not normally given to criticism but he looked at Alan Woking. "Thanks for giving him a piece of your mind, Alan. What he needs is a good talking to by the foreman."

"What he needs, Den, is a swift, hard kick up the arse, that's what he needs," growled Alan. "How's his fireman ever going to learn to be a driver, if the bastard won't let him off the shovel?"

The question was rhetorical. Dennis nodded; he felt that he was fortunate in having Ernie Birthisel as his own driver. Ernie was both considerate and good-natured, and frequently tried to help and advise Dennis. This consideration, however, worked both ways. Ernie was not always in the best of health; he was over 60 years old and was now confined to the shunting link. He occasionally became breathless when climbing up into the cab, so Dennis always made sure that he was up there first to give Ernie a hand and pull him up. Ernie loved his job and was worried that any weakness might be seen as grounds for dismissal from the company.

On entering a cab for a shift, Driver Jones always drew a chalk line across the cab floor and pointed to it when Fireman Winter climbed in. "You move across that line into my side of the cab, and you're done for!" he'd say. "I'll make sure you'll stay a fireman for the rest of your life!"

Bill Winter had three children and couldn't afford to lose his job so did as he was told, but he was always very glad when a shift had him occasionally paired with a different driver.

The confrontation in the enginemen's cabin had apparently made no impression on Huw Jones. Having picked up a Precursor at Manchester's Longsight shed for a Swansea express, they would take it as far as Shrewsbury where there would be a crew change.

By the time they reached Nantwich, Bill Winter was feeling very weary indeed. He'd had no break in firing since they had left the shed in Manchester, and the locomotive of the heavy express had needed every ounce of coal that he was able to put into its firebox. Furthermore, after a week of this heavy train which they had crewed from Manchester to Shrewsbury and back, he was no longer capable of any sustained work.

"Come on you lazy bugger," Huw Jones shouted at him, "We're ten minutes behind time! We're going to be late in Shrewsbury and this'll go on your slate, I'll make sure of that! I'm not getting the blame for my fireman's idleness!"

Bill Winter didn't reply, he just shovelled the coal into the firebox. He didn't even have the energy or will to check where the coal was going; he just thrust shovelful after shovelful into the firebox, while his driver sat on the wooden seat with the regulator in his right hand, keeping the speed right up.

Passing Wem, Driver Jones pulled out his watch and checked it once more. "Hmm, still three minutes down," he muttered to himself, "A bit more speed and we might make it in time – save a bit of paperwork, and..." he turned to his fireman, "keep you out of trouble, although you don't deserve it!"

Bill wasn't listening; he was now shovelling automatically and the train was racing along on the Shrewsbury approaches. Two miles from Shrewsbury station, however, as he turned to pick up more coal from the tender, Bill hesitated and then gradually bent down, dropping his shovel before slumping to the cab floor.

Shocked, Driver Jones stared at his fireman and yelled, "What the hell are you doin' you idle sod? This is no time for a kip! Get shovelling!"

Bill Winter didn't move. He was out cold.

Driver Jones leaned down to grab his arm, but his fireman was clearly unable to rise. Jones opened the firebox doors and glanced inside; the fire was burning quite well and could be left, he thought, until they reached Shrewsbury, where he could get assistance. He thought he might even manage to reach the station on time and he would then have clear evidence as to how useless his fireman was.

He pondered for a moment on whether he would get a commendation for managing the express on his own while his fireman was sick; he could always claim Winter had collapsed passing Nantwich and he, Driver Jones, had managed alone from there. Getting the train into the station on time would be the icing on the cake, so he kept the speed up, even though he knew the fire would need serious attention at Shrewsbury. By then, he thought, that would be a new fireman's problem.

Occupied with these pleasant thoughts, Driver Jones did not realise quite how close he was to the sharp curve immediately before entering the station. He had to drop the regulator quickly and apply the emergency brakes. Even then, the train rounded the curve at a far higher speed than the restriction permitted and only by some miracle did not derail.

A station porter watching the train commented to his colleague, "The way those North-Western drivers belt round that corner, one day one of 'em's going to come off!"

He spoke prophetically; the following year one did, with a considerable loss of life.

Driver Jones, however, was lucky. Fireman Winter was immediately taken to the First Aid room at Shrewsbury's LNWR Coleham shed and a replacement fireman worked the return run as far as Crewe, where Driver Jones was called in to explain why he had almost derailed an express outside Shrewsbury station, and why Fireman Winter was in such an exhausted state that he had collapsed.

Huw Jones began his explanation that his fireman had a tendency to laziness but was interrupted sharply by the shed foreman.

"Frankly, Driver Jones, I don't believe a word you say. Every other driver claims Fireman Winter is a hard-working and conscientious man, whereas you have long had a reputation for bullying your firemen. Furthermore, for almost causing a serious accident with an express, by rights you should face instant dismissal from the company. However, I have discretionary powers and am very short of enginemen and so I am prepared to offer you only a demotion to fireman."

"But sir! I had to cope on my own from Nantwich!"

"I see, so you chose to ignore the safety of the train and not stop to get help for your fireman at either Whitchurch or Wem? Not good enough, Jones. Now, do you accept my offer as fireman?"

Jones nodded, shocked. At the age of 57, he had no real choice.

"Good, your new shift starts tomorrow."

The next morning, Fireman Jones checked the roster board to see what his shift was to be.

9.38 Crewe - Carlisle, passr.	*Guard: F. Singleton*
	Driver: A. Woking
	Fireman: H. Jones

He closed his eyes and grimaced. *He was firing to Driver Alan bloody Woking!*

14 - The Lunatic (October 1907)

Fireman Johnny Winslowe was tired and hungry; the shift had been a hard one although he and his driver Patrick O'Leary had not covered too many miles; they had spent most of the day shunting in Willesden Yard. The weather had been miserable, raining hard all day, and they had suffered problems with their locomotive. It was an elderly Ramsbottom 0-6-0T special tank engine whose protection for the crew was minimal; there was only a partial roof over their heads, so they got thoroughly drenched. Neither cylinder was steam-tight and both were leaking. Consequently, Johnny had been hard pressed to keep steam up, even for shunting duties. His only consolation was that the constant shovelling had at least prevented him from getting too cold.

His driver did not have this dubious advantage in the weather and could be heard from time to time muttering what Johnny took to be obscenities in Erse. Clearly the locomotive should have been attended to by the fitters, but for some reason had escaped the shed foreman's attention.

"As soon as the shift's over, Johnny me bhoy, we'll get this bloody engine seen to. I don't see why any other poor divil should have to drive it like this."

Johnny could only agree wholeheartedly; his arms were aching from use of the shovel. A shunting turn would not normally require heavy firing and many firemen were glad of the chance to take things easy, even if the weather was against them. On this occasion, he'd not been so lucky.

However, before their shift ended, things took a turn for the better. First, the rain stopped, and then the yardmaster came and climbed into their cab.

"A transfer freight has arrived at Liverpool Street from Ely and Cambridge. It has four LNWR vans and the Great Eastern says they can get them to Bow Goods on the North London Railway where we can pick them up and bring them here, so pick up Goods Guard Brian Simpson and a brake van and off you go, lads."

"Nice break from shunting, Johnny, let's hope the engine can get us there and back," said Patrick as they set off.

Once in Bow yard, they detached their brake van and told Brian he had time to boil his kettle for a quick brew while they went to find the North London Railway yardmaster. He directed them to a siding where an elderly shunter was carrying a shunting pole.

"That's Ernie, he'll show you where your vans are," said the yardmaster. "Don't worry about him; I know he looks 95, but looks are deceiving – he's only 89!"

Patrick chuckled. "Only a sprog then, is he?"

They pulled up next to Ernie and Johnny leaned out of the cab and called down to him, "Where are our four LNWR vans?"

Ernie looked up, "What do they look like?"

Johnny was impatient. "They look like LNWR vans – they're grey and have LNWR in bloody great letters on the side."

Ernie didn't move. "I dunno," he muttered, "Yer better ask someone else."

As he spoke another shunter walked past him and said, "Two white diamonds, Ernie."

"Ah, them! Oh yeah they're over yonder," Ernie pointed to a siding where the vans stood at the head of a train of assorted goods vehicles.

"Two white..? What the hell's he talking about, Mr O'Leary?" In their cab, Johnny stared at Patrick in bafflement.

Patrick opened the regulator and the engine gently moved off towards the points, to be switched to the siding where the vans were.

"Two white diamonds?" smiled Patrick, "Ah yes, if you look carefully, ye'll see that many LNWR goods vehicles have two white diamonds on them as well as the letters."

Johnny was still puzzled. "Why?"

Patrick smiled again, "Yer a bright lad; go on – 'ave a guess."

Johnny shook his head. "I haven't got the faintest idea."

"In the early days, most of the railway companies didn't always use their company letters; they put their own sets of symbols on the vehicles so shunters and others could tell which vehicles belonged to which companies. This was helpful for the company employees who couldn't read; and some of them still can't."

"Can't read?" Johnny was astonished.

"Th' auld fellah is probably about 70; likely born about 1840. Lots o' kids didn't go to school then. He's even older than the LNWR itself an'... *what th' hell?*" Patrick stared through the spectacle plate window ahead as he saw a man gyrating in a slow dance in the middle of the track they were proceeding along. Patrick blew the whistle frantically and the man turned, glared at the approaching engine, and stepped aside only a fraction of a second before they reached him.

"What d'ye think ye're doin', ye daft bugger!" yelled Patrick out of the cab as they passed the man, his Irish accent suddenly broader in his fright. "Ye nearly got yerself killt, so ye did!"

A few moments later there was a loud *clunk!* as a piece of coal hit the backhead between the two crewmen and dropped to the cab floor. They turned and saw the same man shaking his fist at them before stepping back onto the track and commencing his odd dance again. Patrick shook his head at Johnny, tapping himself above the ear to indicate what he thought of the man's mental state.

"Let me go and grab him, so that we can…" began Johnny, but Patrick shook his head.

"No, leave him be, it'll only make us late. We'll just report it and the lads here can deal with him."

They picked up the four LNWR vans, crossed the goods yard to the siding where they had left their brake van, and collected it with their guard.

"Righto Johnny, I'll go and tell the yardmaster about that loony while you get the brake van coupled up."

The yardmaster listened, frowning. "That sounds like Daft Eric you're talking about. Short fellow with long, blond hair that needs a proper cut?"

"Aye, that's him."

"He's usually pretty harmless and I've never seen him on the tracks before. I've certainly never heard of him being violent."

"Well he threw a piece of coal at us when we blew the whistle for him to get off the track."

"I'll tell the lads here to keep an eye open for him; he might have forgotten to take his medicine. Thanks for the warning."

Patrick went back to the engine, which Johnny had by now coupled up to the brake van and the four other vans.

"I've warned the guard about that daft bloke, just in case he sees him," Johnny said, looking back towards the brake van. "And the guard's ready; he's just waved his flag."

"Fast work," commented Patrick as he lifted the regulator gently to take the train away out of the yard to Willesden. They moved across the yard throat and onto the main line leading to the North London Railway.

"Funny," muttered Patrick a while after they had cleared the yard and were back on the main line, "Even with a light load, the engine's not pulling properly. It wasn't so bad as we came into Bow Junction."

The engine was working hard but not getting much movement from its short train, and it gradually ground to a stop. Patrick growled another imprecation in Erse as he tried to get the train moving again, but it wouldn't budge. Johnny glanced back along the train and saw a movement on the track between the last van and the brake van.

"Hey Mr O'Leary, there's someone on the track near the brake van!"

"What?" Patrick also looked back. "By all the saints, it's that Daft Eric fellah! How the divil did he get there? Run back and warn the guard, then get that gormless bugger out of the way! Tie the sod up if you have to."

Johnny ran back to the brake van and climbed in. As he was talking to the guard, he caught sight of Daft Eric on the other side and saw him run along the track towards the engine. Johnny ran back to the engine and climbed into the cab.

"The guard didn't see him," he gasped, "but I think Daft Eric had climbed into one of the vans in Bow yard."

"Jasus, Mary and Joseph! And where is he now?"

"He was running this way!"

Patrick thought for a moment then said, "We can't go any further with a madman running loose. I'm going to move slowly up to that signal box and let the bobby there know what's happened. But before I move, just go back to the brake van and warn Brian to look out for the mad bugger. I bet that stupid spalpeen put the vans' brakes on. No wonder we couldn't get up any speed."

As Patrick had suspected, the vans' brakes were all on. Johnny ran along the train, lifted the four brake levers and waved to his driver. Patrick eased the train slowly forward and drove gently the 300 yards to the signal box. Here they reported the problem to the bobby, who telephoned Bow yard to explain the delay. The police turned up in the form of a constable and a sergeant and began the search for Daft Eric but to no avail.

Later, back in Willesden yard, Johnny and Patrick reported the day's events to the yard foreman, as well as the condition of their tank engine, which clearly needed to go back to the works for maintenance.

"Did you search the empty vans before you left?" asked the foreman.

"Johnny checked them when we first stopped; that's when he saw the loony running alongside the train."

"But did you check the vans again before you left?"

"Er, no. As we were running late like, we thought the coppers would do that."

"Coppers aren't railwaymen – they wouldn't know how to check the vans' doors properly. You'd better go and check 'em again."

Patrick sent Johnny back to the vans, and he saw that one of them had an open door. He reported this to the foreman, who was unhappy to hear it.

"Sounds like we might have that fellow here in our yard somewhere. You two had better have a scout round and see if you can find him before he does anything really daft."

"But," said Patrick, "we're supposed to be off duty now."

"You two are the only two who know what he looks like," the foreman pointed out, adding in a voice that brooked no argument, "Find him."

While they were talking, a loud crash came from the yard. The three men ran out of the foreman's office to see two trucks derailed, having been shunted down the wrong siding. The shunter turned to the foreman and shouted, "It warn't me, sir. I'd set the points correctly!"

The driver of the shunting engine called out, "I saw 'im, sir; it was some little long-haired tyke; he come and switched the points after I'd uncoupled the trucks; then 'e buggered orf!"

The foreman looked at Patrick and Johnny, "Your Daft Eric's been busy already. I'm going to telephone the police. You see if you can find him."

With that, he hurried back into his office.

Johnny and Patrick split up and began to search through the yard. As they did so, a slow goods moved out and onto the main line eastbound towards Bow on the North London Line. A head with long, blond hair popped up out of one of the wagons and waved at them, grinning.

Daft Eric was leaving Willesden yard and going home.

15 - The Irish Question (July 1909)

The boat train express from Euston to Liverpool had a Precursor 4-4-0 as train engine and an 0-6-2T tank engine banking it up the gradient out of the main departure platform. Patrick O'Leary and Johnny Winslowe were working hard but it was clear that all was not well. Nearing the top, Fireman Winslowe was needing to put in extra effort to maintain the initial head of steam - on a locomotive renowned for ease of firing and responsive steaming. By Watford he was shovelling continuously and they were already two minutes late running through Tring Cutting.

"Don't know what the trouble is," muttered Patrick. "Everything seems to be working fine."

He looked first into the firebox.

"That fire's not right!" he said, looking at his fireman, and then he peered at the coal in the tender

"Ah, not your fault, Johnny me lad, we've been given some duff coal."

"What's wrong with the coal?"

"I think we've been given the slow goods coal, not the express engine coal." Expresses were given higher quality coal in order to get passengers to their stations on time – goods trains were treated with a little less urgency. Patrick continued, "Don't worry, I'll give ye a hand with the firing."

"Thank you, Mr O'Leary."

Thereafter, Patrick began to drive the engine with supreme skill, tapping into the great reserve of power from the locomotive to compensate for the short supply of steam. Occasionally he gave Johnny a turn at firing and, with it, some advice on how to manage poor coal - for the deliberately violent blast lifted the partly burnt coal fumes through the flue tubes, thus preventing the firebed 'clagging up' and choking the fire. However, this technique called for a lot more shovelling.

They were still six minutes late arriving at Rugby, at which Patrick was unhappy. He began to push the engine as hard as he could while occasionally giving Johnny advice and taking a turn on the firing, with the result that, as they pulled into Stafford, he glanced at the platform clock and turned to Johnny, beaming.

"There y'are, Johnny me bhoy, right time!"

Johnny looked over at the clock on the opposite platform and said with a grin, "No, Mr O'Leary, we're three hours early!"

"*What?*"

Johnny pointed to the clock; it showed ten minutes past nine.

Patrick laughed, "Someone's in trouble; they forgot to wind that clock up! Ye'd better find a porter and tell him. Passengers'll be very confused. Ye've plenty of time; we've got a ten minute wait for the connection from Birmingham. Meanwhile," he continued, climbing down onto the track from the cab, "I'll just have a quick look at the motion; it feels odd."

Johnny checked that the brake was firmly screwed down before he climbed down to warn a porter about the clock. On returning to the cab, he was checking the gauges once more, before sitting down for a short break, when he heard a voice from the platform calling. He looked down and saw a middle-aged man peering into the cab.

"You the fireman then?" the man was smartly dressed and had a well-modulated Oxford accent. *Obviously a toff*, thought Johnny.

"That's right, sir."

"Where's your driver?"

"Mr O'Leary's checking something on the engine; he'll be back very soon."

"O'Leary, you said; Irishman, is he?"

"Yes sir."

"My name is Mottershead, Colonel Mottershead. I'm going back to Ireland; I've a property there. Don't like the Irish; lazy and incompetent, the lot of 'em; and they'll cheat you as soon as look at you."

Johnny fervently hoped that his driver hadn't heard this. But Patrick was climbing the steps back into the cab and he paused and frowned before continuing his ascent. He winked at Johnny and walked over to the platform side of the cab. He had an unusually subservient expression on his face.

"Kin Oi help ye, sorr?" he asked with a ludicrously exaggerated accent.

"Are you taking this train to Liverpool? I need to catch the ferry to Dublin."

"Indeed sorr, dat's what we're doin'."

"Liverpool Riverside?"

"Oi t'ink so, sorr."

"You don't sound certain?"

"One moment sorr, Oi'll check in me book." Patrick took out his train journal and pretended to peruse it.

"Dat's roight, sorr, Liverpool Riverside, arrival 2.14."

As they were talking, Johnny noticed that the Birmingham connecting train had arrived. He pointed this out unobtrusively to his driver who nodded and muttered out of the corner of his mouth, "Just check for the guard's flag, we might need to get away a bit smartish."

Patrick leaned out to speak once more to the man on the platform.

"Anyt'ing else Oi can help ye wid, sorr?"

The man glanced at the clock on the platform and at the one opposite.

"Certainly there is, my man." He had a triumphant smirk on his face. "The clock on this platform says it's 12.32, whereas the clock on the opposite platform says it's 9.17. Can you explain why?"

Johnny, looking back down the train, saw the guard's green flag and nodded once more to Patrick, who glanced at the two clocks and replied, "Indeed ye're roight sorr, to be sure. But den if dey both said the same toime, well, we wouldn't be after needin' two o' dem, would we?"

He gave the whistle chain a quick tug and took hold of the regulator. Colonel Mottershead stared, frowning, at the two clocks, puzzled. Then, noticing that the train was beginning to move, ran back to his carriage to make an undignified jump into his compartment.

"Ignorant swine!" muttered Patrick to Johnny as they left Stafford station on their way to Crewe next stop.

"I hope he doesn't complain to management," commented Johnny, hoping that Patrick's sense of humour hadn't got him into trouble. Insulting a member of the public was taken seriously by the LNWR.

"What did he call us Irish, Johnny?" asked Patrick.

"Lazy and incompetent," replied Johnny.

"There y'are then; if he complains about me, I'll take him to court. I've got you as a witness, so I have."

Later, as they were nearing Crewe, Patrick's face had an unusually serious expression on it. "That pompous ass was right about the problem with Ireland; there certainly is laziness, incompetence and cheating there, but it's not the Irish, it's the British government and many of the landowners."

"The landowners?" said Johnny, surprised.

"Aye, a lot of them are English and don't care about their poor farmworker tenants. They've learned nothin' from the Potato Famine of the 1840s when hundreds of thousands of us either starved or migrated. Take my advice Johnny, and don't go to Ireland!"

"Why ever not?" After working with Patrick, Johnny had been thinking of going to Ireland to see if the Irish were generally as good-natured as his driver. He had also heard that Ireland was a green and beautiful country.

"Because sooner or later the English will be forced to leave; they won't go willingly so they will be kicked out – and it'll be bloody!"

Johnny shook his head, "I think there'll be trouble with Germany before there's trouble in Ireland."

"Don't you believe it!" Patrick was deadly serious, "There are Irishmen who would be delighted if England and Germany went to war; they would join the Germans to be able to kick the English out of Ireland."

"They'd turn traitor?" Johnny couldn't believe his ears.

"Traitor?" Patrick queried. "If your country was occupied by foreigners and you fought them, would you be a traitor?"

"Foreigners?" Johnny couldn't believe his ears. "But Ireland's ours!"

"Don't you know your history, Johnny Winslowe? Your kings took Ireland; we want it back!"

Johnny was silent; he hadn't thought of it that way before.

At Crewe he saw Colonel Mottershead hurry along the platform to an office and reappear a few minutes later, just before departure.

Hope he hasn't complained to authority, Johnny thought as they got the right away and moved off. But Johnny had other matters on his mind as they approached Warrington. Their Precursor was steaming very poorly, and although Patrick had given Johnny a hand with the shovelling, things were not going well. They were losing more time and this could have serious effects on passengers who had arranged to travel on by sea. They had to request assistance for the remaining part of the run to Liverpool. Fortunately the Widnes pilot engine, an elderly Jumbo 2-4-0, was coaled up and available and the rest of the journey was made without any further loss of time. Nevertheless, their arrival at Riverside Station was 25 minutes down; grounds for many complaints from passengers and maritime officials, which all reflected badly on the service provided by the London and North Western Railway.

For Patrick O'Leary, the matter was considerably more serious. It appeared that Colonel Mottershead was both well-known and influential in Liverpool. He had registered a serious complaint by telegraph from Crewe and had accused Driver O'Leary of both insulting language to an important passenger and dereliction of duty in allowing the train to be late. The official waiting on the platform instructed Driver O'Leary and Fireman Winslowe to immediately catch a tram to Lime Street and to make themselves available to an investigating officer within the hour.

"This is a very serious business," they were told sternly. "It seems that you have brought the company into disrepute. However, the matter will not be resolved here; it will be dealt with in Euston. Driver O'Leary, you are suspended as of now and you and Fireman Winslowe will report to the Camden foreman tomorrow afternoon at two pm sharp."

The office at the Euston headquarters of the LNWR held four officials, including the Camden shed foreman. The latter glanced at Patrick and shook his head very slightly. Patrick and Johnny were sitting nervously in front of the big desk. The Divisional Superintendent in charge of the case looked up from the sheet of paper he had been reading, took off his pince-nez, and glared at the two enginemen.

"Have you read Colonel Mottershead's report?"

"No sir," Patrick tried hard to reduce his Irish accent.

"You'd better read it," the Superintendent said and passed it across. Patrick read it quickly and gave it to Johnny, who also read it and placed it back on the desk.

"Well?"

Patrick's face was red, "'Tis a pack o' lies, sir, so it is!"

"Your view, Fireman Winslowe?"

"I must agree with my driver, Mr O'Leary, sir," Johnny spoke firmly, "that's not what happened."

"There is no veracity in the description?" The Superintendent addressed Patrick once more.

"Er - pardon, sorr?" Patrick's accent was accentuated by his nervousness.

"There is no truth at all in the report?"

Patrick hesitated, "Well, sorr, I did have a little joke wid him."

The Superintendent looked questioningly at Johnny who nodded, "It was a harmless joke sir, and not at all offensive."

The official turned his head to the Camden shed foreman, "How would you rate Driver O'Leary, Mr Blenkinsop?"

"He's one of my best and most reliable drivers, sir."

"And would you accept his word?"

"On a serious matter such as this one, sir; I would, most certainly."

"Hmm - so it's the enginemen's word against the Colonel's?"

"No sir, it's not. I spoke on the telephone to the Stafford stationmaster this morning. He is familiar with complaints about the Colonel, who is frequently both arrogant and rude to the station staff there. Furthermore, sir, as for the late arrival in Liverpool, that is hardly down to the engine crew; the locomotive was coaled in error with unsuitable coal."

"I see," the Superintendent paused for a moment then wrote something on Patrick's work record before announcing his verdict. "Driver O'Leary, I have recorded 'Undue levity to a passenger; one day's loss of pay. No further action'. You may go."

Outside the office, Patrick shook the shed foreman's hand, "T'ank you, sorr, you've saved me job."

The shed foreman shook his head again, this time in amusement. "Don't play silly buggers with important passengers, Patrick; learn to keep your gob shut. And keep Fireman Winslowe with you at all times."

It was some weeks later that Patrick showed Johnny an Irish newspaper with a report on the murder of a local landowner, Colonel Lawrence Mottershead, who'd had the reputation of being 'firm' with his tenants. He had been found on his land one morning with his throat cut. The coroner had found a verdict of 'Murder by a person or persons unknown'.

16 - The Racing Drivers (November 1911)

Passing Abergele, Albert Jenkins, driver of the 4-6-0 Experiment class locomotive taking the up *Irish Mail* on its way to Euston, frowned.

His fireman glanced over, "What's the trouble, Mr Jenkins?"

"The trouble, Doug, is that our pilot is not pulling its weight," Albert replied, "And we're having to do most of the work."

The pilot engine was a 4-6-0 Prince of Wales class and it was not assisting the heavy express as much as it ought to have been. In fact, the train was travelling rather more slowly along the North Wales coast than the timetable demanded.

"At this rate we'll only be crawling through Prestatyn," commented Albert, annoyed, as they passed through Rhyl at low speed.

In the event, they did not crawl through Prestatyn; they stopped on the fast up line. The driver of the pilot climbed down from his cab and came over to the train engine.

"What's up, Eric?" asked Albert. "We can't stop here; we're non-stop to Chester, Crewe and Euston."

"We've got problems, Albert. She's not pulling at all well. I'm going to have to fail her."

"Can you get her as far as Chester then, Eric? Neither here nor Dyserth will be able to help and Rhyl shed is unlikely to have a decent replacement engine. But if we tell them here, they can telephone Chester for an express engine to be ready."

"Yes, I think she'll make it to Chester. I'll contact the bobby here and he can pass the message on."

Eric Handley hurried over to the nearby signal box to inform the bobby then returned to his engine. The whistle sounded and they were off again. 50 minutes later they pulled in at Chester's Number Ten platform and the Prince of Wales uncoupled and moved slowly off to the LNWR shed for attention. Albert Jenkins' fireman, Douglas Lawson, slipped down to couple up the replacement engine, a 4-4-0 Jubilee class, while Albert leaned on the cabside and watched the passengers.

An attractive young lady was sitting on a bench with her luggage by her side as a couple in their 30s passed her. The man glanced at the young lady and his companion poked him sharply in the side with her umbrella. Albert picked up some of their conversation and found it highly diverting.

"Control yourself, you lecherous beast!" said the lady with mock severity, "I saw you looking at that girl's ankles!"

"I am controlling myself - I didn't touch her!" replied the man indignantly.

"Well you're still a lecherous beast!"

"Of course I am; I'm a bloke. All us blokes are lecherous beasts; it's not that we're evil – it's the way we're built." But what his wife - she was clearly his wife - replied, Albert missed as they walked on. He was disappointed; he would have liked to hear her rejoinder.

By this time, Doug had returned to their cab; the pilot was coupled on and ready for the off. Albert took out his watch from his waistcoat and looked at it. "Does the driver of the pilot know we are now 37 minutes behind time?"

"Yes, Mr Jenkins, he's keen to make up as much as possible."

"Do you know who he is?"

"I think he said his name was Rawlings."

"Not Ernest Rawlings?"

"He didn't tell me his Christian name."

Albert smiled, "If it's Ernie Rawlings, we don't need to worry. I know Ernest; he hates being late. But I don't envy his fireman!"

By the time they stopped at Crewe, Albert had no doubt that Ernest Rawlings was driving their pilot; the Jubilee was clearly in good nick, they had already regained six of the minutes and were now only just over half an hour behind time. He didn't have time to chat to the driver of the pilot, however, because they got the right away quickly as the passengers had been chivvied on board by the station staff. No railwayman likes late trains, especially crack expresses like the *Irish Mail*, and the pilot engine had begun to move the instant the guard had started to unroll his green flag. Albert hurriedly lifted his regulator to prevent a snatch on the couplings between the pilot and the train engine; this could break the couplings and part the train. By the time the guard was waving his green flag, they were already accelerating.

Albert grinned at his fireman. Douglas looked back at him questioningly; he didn't know whether he was going to be exhilarated or worn out. Probably both, he suspected.

"We're in for an interesting time, Doug my lad!" said Albert.

Roaring through Stafford, Doug knew he was in for an exciting run. Both locomotives were running smoothly and at high speed, and they had already regained several more minutes. South of Stafford, Doug glanced out of the cab side once he saw that the fire was burning well and didn't need any more coal for a few minutes. His eyes blinked as he noticed a strange looking bird gliding ahead of them. It seemed to be curiously stiff, and he pointed it out to his driver. Albert also stared out as they began to get closer.

"That's not a bird," said Albert. "I think that's a flying machine and we're catching it up." He leaned out of the cab, pulling the whistle chain to draw the attention of the pilot engine's crew to the unusual sight.

"I've never seen one of them before," replied Doug. "What do they call them: airy-planes?"

"Something like that; I think 'aeroplanes' is the right word. I've never seen one either."

They were rapidly overtaking the aircraft and, as it was flying in the same direction as they were travelling, they got a good look at it as they swept past it.

Albert looked back along the train and laughed. "Have a look at our train! Half the passengers have their heads out of the windows. I bet most of them haven't seen an aeroplane before either."

"We should charge them extra for the entertainment," Doug turned his attention back to the firebox. He had been firing long enough to know very well that the fire in a steam locomotive could quickly develop holes. These had to be filled with coal before the driver began to lose the steam which he needed. He also knew that while Albert Jenkins was a good and considerate driver to work for, if he was unhappy with his fireman's efforts, the fireman would know all about it very soon. He quickly filled up one or two low points in the fire bed before they could affect the steaming. This was proving to be one of the hardest days firing that he could remember.

By this time, the aircraft was well back as the express was travelling at about 80 or 85 miles an hour; the aircraft had been flying at about 30 or so.

"I wouldn't like to be in one of them," commented Albert, glancing back at it. "It'd be like being in a motor car, except that if the engine stopped you'd be dead. My kids have got a box kite that looks a bit like that and when the wind drops, so does the kite!"

They continued racing south and Doug watched with amusement as they roared through Rugby, blowing hats and umbrellas around among the waiting passengers. Albert pulled out the big watch from his waistcoat and looked at it.

"We've made up 19 minutes," he grinned, "If we keep going like this, we might even arrive on time at Euston!"

Doug didn't answer; he was busy shovelling and hoping they wouldn't run out of coal. The engine was eating it up almost as fast as he could throw it into the firebox.

Albert noticed his fireman's worried expression and looked in the tender at the amount of coal left and at the water gauge. "Hmm," he muttered, "Might have to be a bit careful."

By Tring they were both getting concerned. The water level in the gauge was getting low, as was the pile of coal in the tender. Reaching Watford Junction, however, Albert realised that they had just enough to reach Euston, but the engine began to work harder. He frowned. What was the problem? Looking back along the train he couldn't see anything amiss. They were still speeding but the train was slowing and they were very thankful when they reached the top of Camden Bank; it was now downhill into Euston. Thankfully, they rolled slowly in under the great station roof, eased their way into Number Two main arrival platform and stopped gently, several yards from the buffer stops. They were three minutes late. Albert climbed down from the cab and walked to the pilot engine to speak to the driver.

"Hello Ernie, many thanks for the help! We left Chester 37 minutes late and we're now only three minutes down; well done!"

But Ernest wasn't smiling. "Come up, Bert," he said, "come and look at this!"

Albert climbed up and Ernest Rawlings opened the firebox doors. The fire in the Jubilee was almost out; Ernest looked in the tender. There wasn't a single lump of coal in it.

"We ran out just before Watford; since then you've been pushing us as well," explained Ernest.

"Ah, so that's it!" replied Albert, "We noticed the train getting heavy about then. Still, we made it. At Tring I thought we might not!"

"Have you got enough steam to tow us up to Camden?" asked Ernest. "We'll never make it up the bank to the shed on our own, and if I call for a tow from the station pilot I'll never hear the last of it!"

"I think so, especially after what you two have done for us. Mind you, there'll have to be a couple of pints in it for me and my fireman in the pub tonight. Poor lad, he's just about knackered; I don't think the beers will touch the sides of his throat as they go down."

Ernest looked at his own fireman, who nodded.

"You're on!" he grunted, adding with a smile, "Mind you, I had an easy time after Watford Junction!"

"Yes," said Albert to Ernest's fireman, "But you had better nip to Doug and ask him for a couple of shovels of coal to put in your own tender; it doesn't look good if you arrive with it completely empty. Quick now," he said, glancing down the platform.

Ernest's fireman hurried to see Doug and cadge some coal. As they were talking, the postal officials were already unloading the mail from the vans in the train, and they saw uniformed authority striding along the platform towards them.

The platform inspector stopped in front of the two drivers, nodding to himself and jotting in his notebook. "Albert Jenkins and Ernest Rawlings; I might have known it," he chuckled. "We heard from Chester that you were running 37 minutes behind time with the *Mail*, and now you're only three minutes down. That was fine work lads and it's noted; but I bet both your firemen won't forget the run in a hurry! I'd like to see the contents of your tender, Bert!"

Albert guided him to his locomotive and showed him the few lumps of coal left there. The inspector went to Ernest's engine and saw much the same. "I'm glad you two have both got some coal left, even if it's not very much. It looks bad when you arrive empty. Oh, and Ernest, you can tell your fireman he can put those shovelfuls of coal back in Bert's tender now!"

He turned away with a grin.

17 - The Cleaner (October 1913)

Charge-hand Lennie Hamble surveyed the young lad standing in front of him, outside the door to his office in the LNWR locomotive shed in Banbury. He saw a tall boy with ill-fitting clothes and a diffident manner, but he also noticed that the lad's eyes were alert as he glanced around the big shed, taking in the details.

"You're Julian Connell, I take it, just appointed to help us clean these fine engines you see around us?"

"Er – ye... yessir," replied the boy.

"Very well. Now, some words of advice: do what your betters tell you, work diligently, and keep your nose clean. The lads here will help you; they were all new once, but watch out for tricks. Don't fall for a request to get some left-handed nuts or long skyhooks! Oh, and, er," he paused, "Don't tell them your first name; you'll get teased."

"Yes sir," said Julian.

"See that tall lad by the cab of that 2-4-0?"

"Er - what's a 2-4-0, sir?"

"That's how we classify our engines, lad. A 2-4-0 has two small front wheels, four big driving wheels, and none behind them. That one belongs to the Precedent class of engines; very fast in their day, but a bit dated by now."

"Oh, yes, right, sir."

"The fellow there by the cab is Senior Cleaner McIntosh; he will look after you. Now off you go."

With that, Lennie Hamble went back into his office.

Julian walked over to the Senior Cleaner who was standing near the cab of the big engine, watching another cleaner polishing the cab side. He looked around when he heard Julian's footsteps.

"Ah, the new boy, I believe, Junior Cleaner Connell?"

"Umm, yes."

"You don't sound very sure?"

"Sorry, yes I am Junior Cleaner Connell."

"Glad we got that sorted. Now, your first duty is to learn how to clean engines; you'll need a scouring pad, and an oily rag and some cotton waste. Cleaner Blair here will help you. You can start on this engine's smoke box; that's the front part of the boiler."

He turned to the lad cleaning the cab side, "Show him the ropes,

John, he's new today."

"Right-oh, George." John Blair climbed down from the ladder leaning up against the cab and held out his hand.

"John Blair at your service," he said with a grin, "Welcome to the merry band of cleaners. What's your moniker?"

"Ju- er John Connell," said Julian, remembering just in time not to give his real name.

"Fine then Ju-John; first, we'll get you some cleaning stuff and then I'll show you how to use it."

They went to the stores office where John introduced Julian to the charge-hand and requested the materials Julian would need. Back at the locomotive, John showed Julian how to clean off some of the grime from the smoke-box and then said, "I'll get back to my cleaning and leave you to it, John. Mind you clean the smoke-box thoroughly and don't forget to clean the inside of the chimney as well as the outside. The smoke makes it very dirty."

Julian nodded, climbed up the footplate steps, and began to rub the dirt off the smoke-box. Straightaway he found that he couldn't get the same gleaming finish that John was getting. He eased his way along the footplate to where John was and asked how he could get the same polished finish.

"Oh, no; you won't get a polish on the smoke-box. It has a different matte finish from the rest of the boiler, which is gloss." John walked along to see the square foot that Julian had done and commented, "Yeah, that's fine – you won't get it much better than that. Mr McIntosh will be happy with that."

Julian was relieved and carried on cleaning the rest of the smoke-box sides. He had to mount a ladder to do the rounded top and chimney. He looked anxiously down; he hadn't realised how high it all was from the ground. It was hard work, but already he could see a difference. However, his scouring pad and oily cloth were very dirty, and there was a great deal of dirt transferred from the engine onto his clothing. He noticed several other young cleaners watching him and nodding encouragement. He put his arm round the chimney and cleaned the outside. Then he stood up and put his cloth down inside the chimney. Instantly, his cloth and arm were black with soot, but he persevered and gave the inside a thorough rubbing.

Climbing down again, he was coal-black from waist to head and found himself facing the Senior Cleaner. George McIntosh had a broad grin on his face as he surveyed the young lad.

"I suppose they told you to clean the inside of the chimney, did they?"

Julian nodded.

George shook his head, "I should have warned you about that. The inside of chimneys is never cleaned. Go and clean yourself as best you can."

Julian walked past the other grinning cleaners. *Right, John Blair,* he thought to himself, *you'll pay for that!*

Some days later, he was in a gang of lads cleaning an older engine which had one huge driving wheel each side. Julian thought it looked rather old-fashioned but had to admit that it was impressive, and he had heard that the old single-wheelers, as they were called, could certainly run fast. As he was cleaning, he heard the sound of a speeding train; it was on the nearby Great Western line, which had an adjacent, and larger, station in Banbury. This was apparently an express as it showed no sign of stopping or even slowing down. Julian stared at it as it passed. The engine was another single-wheeler, in Brunswick green with a polished copper dome and a tall chimney with a brass rim. He thought he had never seen a more magnificent engine. It ran past with its dark red coaches, and he began to wonder whether he had joined the right railway; perhaps he should have tried to join the Great Western instead.

He found himself standing next to another figure who was looking at the Great Western engine; it was the charge-hand, Lennie Hamble. "No doubt about it, the Great Western engine looks and runs very well, don't you think?"

"Yes, sir," replied Julian, wishing he could be cleaning such a beautiful engine.

"Yes," continued Mr Hamble, "It's a shame the Great Western changed their coach colours from the brown and cream recently; they looked very good with their green engines. But those engines are not what they seem to be; they are on their way out. The GWR already has much better engines, but just wait till you see what's coming out of our Crewe works very soon! Mind you, we won't see one on this branch; you'd have to go to Bletchley to see one. We only get the older engines. Still, you never know, they might run one down here to trial it."

Julian began to enjoy his work cleaning the engines and was even in the cab occasionally when one of the drivers took his engine out of the shed and into the small station to back onto its train. He took extra efforts to put a sparkle even on the goods engines.

This diligence, however, put him at odds with some of the more lax boys in the cleaning gang.

"Come on Connell, don't put us to shame," John Blair complained one day.

"How am I putting you to shame?" Julian asked.

"Your cleaning makes us look lazy!" replied Blair.

Julian stared at him. "If you don't do your job properly, it's you putting yourself to shame, not me!"

It was freezing cold one January morning when the cleaning gang started work and there were complaints which were properly ignored by George McIntosh.

"Never mind the weather," he commented, pointing out the engine they were to start cleaning, "If you rub hard and clean well you'll soon get warm again."

John Blair rushed quickly into the cab before anyone else could get there, opened the firebox door, and wriggled in to clean out all remaining ash and clinker. Cleaning the firebox was a choice job in winter; it was a scramble to get inside, but it was cosy and warm compared to working outside on the boiler.

When Julian saw what John was up to, he smiled to himself; he could see a chance to get even with Blair on the matter of the chimney on his first day. After the gang outside had completed the boiler, they were due for a lunch break. Julian crept quietly into the cab and peeped inside the firebox; as he suspected, John Blair was sitting inside, enjoying a smoke, while his box of sandwiches were placed conveniently outside on the firebox shelf. Julian shut the fire door gently, dropping the locking bar in place, and joined the rest of the gang with their sandwiches. There was a muffled yell from the firebox unheard by all in the chatter over lunch.

After the lunch half hour, George McIntosh came round to chivvy the lads back to work. As he rounded them up, he heard a thumping noise from the cab. He climbed up and opened the firebox door to see John Blair climb out. "Some bugger locked me in," the boy said angrily, "I've not had my lunch yet!"

"Lunch break's over, John my lad," said George. "It's back to work for you!"

The other boys chuckled. They had seen how John Blair had grabbed the firebox job before they could toss a coin for it, and had no sympathy for him.

A few weeks later, Julian recalled the prophetic words of charge-hand Hamble about the better GWR engines. One of their new ones, a Star class 4-6-0, had been sent to Euston on a trial and it had shown itself to be far superior to the best that the LNWR could offer on its main line to Carlisle. He tackled the charge-hand about it.

"Don't you fret about it, lad," answered the latter, "Our Mr Bowen-Cooke has one up his sleeve that'll make even the GWR sit up and take notice. It'll be out in a year or so."

One day, about 12 months later, Julian was called into the charge-hand's office.

"Now then, Cleaner Connell, Senior Cleaner McIntosh tells me that he is very happy with you and feels you are ready to try more advanced work. I understand you have already been on minor firing duties in the yard here?"

"Yes sir, a few times."

"Good, well tomorrow we are going to send you to Bletchley on a firing turn with a regular fireman to see that you don't do anything silly."

The run to Bletchley the next day was uneventful, and Julian's firing met with approval from the regular fireman, who was watching him closely. A few more similar firing turns saw Julian promoted to Passed Cleaner, which meant he could now officially fire under the supervision of an experienced driver.

While waiting at Bletchley for the return to Banbury some months later, Julian heard a mighty roar as an express tore through the station, hauled by a huge, sparkling engine in its gleaming blackberry paintwork with the red, white and grey lining. With its rake of 'plum and spilt milk' coaches, the whole train made a magnificent sight.

He recalled Lennie Hamble's words. He had been right; it had taken another year, but when the big 4-6-0 *Sir Gilbert Claughton* finally appeared, it demonstrated an impressive ability to handle the heavy expresses. The GWR could keep their Stars and Saints, thought Julian; he had made the right decision. The Premier Line was quite obviously capable of building its own great engines!

18 - The Magistrate (March 1914)

Fireman Winslowe had been saddened to learn that his mate, Driver Patrick O'Leary, was leaving the company to return to his home town of Kilkenny in Ireland. Johnny had valued his time with Patrick and the two had become friends as well as having formed a competent team. Patrick had worked for the LNWR for 23 years and driven for the last eleven, but his sister had written to let him know that their elderly parents in Ireland were unwell. Patrick had thereupon decided to move back with his family to help. His qualifications and experience, as well as a letter of recommendation, had been enough for the Great Southern and Western Railway to offer him a driving position with them as soon as he could learn the road from Dublin to Waterford and Cork.

On checking the enginemen's board, Johnny was horrified to read that he was being paired once more with Bill Hepton, whose time on the lower link had been short – regrettably so, in Johnny's view. Yet Johnny found that his new duties were rather more bearable than he had anticipated; firstly, the shed foreman had quietly assured him that his duty with Driver Hepton would be purely temporary, and, secondly, Bill Hepton turned out to have mellowed somewhat.

Their turn of duty for the next three months involved a morning and an afternoon return run to Bletchley on a semi-fast. One Friday morning, on the platform at Euston, a gentleman in a top hat and other formal attire walked up to them.

"Good morning!" he said cheerfully, addressing Johnny's driver, "All arranged then?"

"Yessir," replied Bill Hepton, "All fixed."

The gentleman nodded, satisfied, walked back to the nearest First Class compartment, and climbed in.

"Who was that, Mr Hepton?" asked Johnny curiously.

"That's Mr Atkinson; he's a magistrate and he travels every Friday to Bletchley and back."

"What's arranged for him?"

"We like to look after him – make sure he gets a good seat, smooth ride home, that sort of thing."

"But he doesn't need us to do that for him."

"Don't worry about it, Johnny."

Johnny was surprised; an earlier Bill Hepton would have snarled at him and told him to mind his own damn business. This time he just carried on with his driving, after a quick glance into the firebox as if to remind his fireman to be about his duties.

On their evening arrival in Euston, while Johnny was down on the track uncoupling the coaches for the station pilot engine to draw them back into the carriage sidings, he noticed his driver talking to their guard. As they talked, Mr Atkinson walked past them with a smile, stopping to hand something to the guard. It looked very much like a banknote, and after he had left, the guard took some coins from his pocket and handed them to Bill Hepton.

As the last passengers from the train passed him, Johnny's attention was distracted from the guard and Driver Hepton by the sight of a very pretty girl. From his position below the platform level, Johnny glimpsed a pair of well-turned ankles, and above the skirt she had a blouse which looked cut low enough for him to wish he had been standing back on the platform. *Even better*, he thought to himself, *on a footbridge looking down.*

He looked away hurriedly with a guilty feeling, telling himself that he was a happily married man and had no cause to be staring down ladies' fronts, no matter how intriguing they were.

Driver Hepton's earlier run-in with the suffragettes and the consequences of his meetings with the Scottish guard and the shed foreman appeared to have had a salutary effect on his attitude in general; his views were expressed in a far more moderate manner in the conversations between driver and fireman. Johnny was relieved that he could now concentrate on his firing technique and he even benefitted from occasional advice received from his driver. From time to time Bill even offered him the regulator for a stretch; an activity that was undoubted evidence of a degree of trust. It was also illegal, and was only practised where both driver and fireman could be sure they would not be observed. Locomotive inspectors and other officials knew it happened and normally turned a blind eye to it, regarding it as informal training for a potential driver. They knew that no driver would risk his career if he didn't trust his fireman. When Johnny found himself on the regulator from time to time it gave a boost to his confidence as a future driver.

One Friday morning, Johnny was on the platform when Mr Atkinson came up to him.

"Good morning, young man; all in order?"

Surprised, Johnny answered, "Yes sir, I believe so."

"Excellent!" beamed the magistrate, and went back to find a compartment.

In their cab, Johnny mentioned this to his driver.

"What did you tell him?" demanded Bill Hepton suspiciously.

"I told him I believed so; but what arrangements are we talking about?"

Driver Hepton stared at him and growled, "I think, Fireman Winslowe, it's time you learned to mind your own bloody business! Look at that hole in your fire!"

"Sorry!" replied Johnny, abashed. He grabbed his shovel to fill the hole which he had allowed to develop. He fervently hoped that Driver Hepton hadn't returned to his previous morose attitude. Nevertheless, later that day on the platform in Bletchley, he kept a wary eye open and sure enough, he saw the magistrate near the rear of the train, once more talking to the guard and, Johnny was sure, money changed hands again.

"Just going to have a word with the guard," said Bill Hepton, "I want to check the train's weight."

As he spoke, the guard's whistle sounded and they saw the green flag waving from the back of the train.

"Bugger!" muttered Driver Hepton.

Johnny wondered what had upset him; it couldn't have been the exact weight of the train. Any experienced driver could count the carriages, look at the passengers on the platform, and make an educated guess at the weight.

Arriving in Euston once more, Johnny observed the magistrate striding past, waving genially at him. As he climbed down from the cab to the platform to uncouple once more, he saw another young girl with a low-cut blouse standing watching him. She grinned and bent down to make sure he caught a clear view of two of her attractions.

"Feast yer eyes on them two, lover boy," she chuckled mischievously, "Lookin's free, but yer can't afford 'em on your pay!"

She stalked off, laughing.

"Saucy baggage!" called Johnny indignantly after her, but all he got in response was an obscene gesture.

Climbing back onto the platform he noticed his driver chatting to the guard and slipping something into his pocket again. Wondering at the coincidence of seeing two girls who were both obviously tarts and the presence of Magistrate Atkinson on the train, Johnny decided to keep his eyes peeled. When another week had passed, he again saw the magistrate travelling on their train to Bletchley and back. He decided that a quiet investigation was warranted. This time, on their arrival back at Euston, another girl of the type his wife would have described as a 'common street girl' walked down the platform, but she paid no attention to him.

For the next two Fridays, Johnny knew the magistrate was travelling on their train for his weekly stint in the local magistrates' court, but this did not explain any connection with a tart, the exchange of money which Johnny was now certain he had seen, or the careful driving of Driver Hepton on Friday evenings. However, one day an opportunity for a discreet reconnaissance presented itself on their return run to Euston; they were held up in Tring and Bill Hepton sent Johnny to the guard to find out what the problem was.

Johnny reached the guard's van, a brake composite, which had two First Class compartments in addition to the luggage section. He glanced in passing into both Firsts, but the magistrate was not in either of them - yet Johnny could have sworn he had seen him enter one of them at Bletchley. The guard's door was open and Johnny entered to query the guard regarding the delay. The guard, however, was nowhere to be seen. Johnny was about to climb out once more when he noticed a section of the luggage van screened off with a curtain. Just outside the curtain was a small desk, upon which rested a top hat and some ladies' underwear. Next to these items hung two coat-hangers; one holding a lady's dress and the other a gentleman's trousers and jacket. From behind the screen, Johnny heard a distinct grunting and gasping which, with some embarrassment, he instantly recognised. He immediately tip-toed back out of the guard's compartment.

Outside, he paused for a moment or two to regain his composure and walked over to the station-master's office. Here he discovered the station-master explaining to the guard that there had been a signalling malfunction which was only causing a minor delay, and Johnny walked back to the cab to inform his driver that they would not be held up for more than another 20 minutes.

After their arrival in Euston, Johnny uncoupled the coaches and then walked back to the guard's van. As the guard had left, he looked inside and observed a fold-up camp bed leaning against the wall; there was no sign of the curtain that he had observed in Tring. Johnny shook his head in disbelief.

I've been firing a travelling brothel! he muttered to himself. *That magistrate has been having it off with a tart every Friday evening, the lecherous old sod! And the guard and my driver have been paid to assist!*

This matter put Johnny firmly on the horns of a dilemma; what should he do about it? It was immoral, almost certainly illegal, and he was technically part of it. What was he to do? He decided to discuss the matter with his wife who, he knew, was generally a source of sensible and practical advice.

"Every Friday evening?" she asked when the matter was broached over the evening meal. Johnny nodded.

"Then you have a week to think it over and come up with something; what about hiding the camp bed?" she suggested.

Johnny wasn't sure how he could do this, but it was at least an idea.

However, the matter sorted itself out quite neatly without Johnny's involvement. On Saturday morning, the enginemen's notice board showed that Johnny's shift had changed. He was now paired with Freddie Blacksmith; a quiet, unassuming driver who was known to encourage his firemen to go for promotion if he felt they were ready.

After a week on shift with him, Freddie told Johnny, "You should be studying the rule book carefully, young Johnny. I reckon you should go for the driver's exam in a year or so."

This comment drove all thoughts about the magistrate out of Johnny's mind for a while until three weeks later he read in the newspaper of a magistrate who had been caught *in flagrante* with a prostitute in a train at Watford. A guard had been sacked and a driver had been severely reprimanded. Johnny felt some slight relief that Bill Hepton hadn't been sacked; after all, he had shown faith in Johnny's driving skill.

"Bill Hepton only drove carefully," explained Freddie, "it was the guard who procured the girls."

"Yes, I suppose so," replied Johnny, "But how did the guard get the girls?"

"The guard's sister works in a Soho brothel."

"How do you know that?" asked Johnny, startled.

"I went out with her once a few years back."

"And..?"

"And you get your mind on the enginemen's rule book," said Freddie firmly.

19 -The Home Front (May 1916)

Fireman Willy Lathrop was pleased; he had just seen the drivers' notice board at Crewe North shed, where he had been transferred the previous year. His application to join the army had been denied on the grounds of the nation's urgent need for experienced railwaymen. But his pleasure was the result of what he saw on the noticeboard. He was to fire his first Claughton class express 4-6-0 locomotive. These were the most powerful passenger locomotives the LNWR had and were only three years old. They could manage the heavy Scottish expresses with ease, although they tended to be greedy on the coal and, consequently, on the firemen's stamina. But still, he thought, the Crewe to Carlisle run was one he had done many times and he knew it well. His first chance at firing a Claughton was welcome, in spite of its reputation for demanding a great deal from the fireman.

His driver, Johnny Winslowe, was equally happy; "Good engines, Claughtons, Willy," he said, "I've driven them often and they won't let you down, even with fourteen on. Mind you, they'll challenge you, I'll give you that, but I'll also give you ten minutes' break after Wigan and another ten after Carnforth so you can get ready for the climb up Tebay and Shap."

"Much obliged, Johnny." Willy still found it hard to get used to calling his new driver by his first name, but Johnny had been insistent about this, arguing that it led to a better understanding between the two crewmen. A good working relationship between a driver and his fireman, claimed Johnny, was essential to get the best out of any locomotive, be it an express passenger train or a local goods, and Willy had driven with enough drivers by this time to know what a difference this could make. A good team (and Willy believed that he and Johnny made a good team) could really make a difference, but time-keeping was frequently upset by the demands of war.

Despite this, it wasn't the war that caused the first of the hold-ups. The weather had been warmer than usual in the last few weeks, with very little rain; consequently, the grass was very dry. A previous freight locomotive had been labouring hard up the hills and sparks from its chimney had set the grass verge alight. This caused an unscheduled stop at Tebay until the fire had been brought under control by the local fire brigade, allowing them to depart. This had held them up and they left Tebay 40 minutes behind schedule. Now deprived of the slight downhill run through Grayrigg and past Tebay to pick up speed and help them tackle the climb up to Shap, the Claughton had its work cut out. Willy had to shovel far harder than he had expected to and the sweat began pouring off his face; his hands were getting very sweaty too, and his grip on the shovel began to loosen. He had put on twelve shovelfuls into the firebox when he paused to wipe his face and hands, but within five minutes they were slippery once more. He paused again to wipe the sweat away as they passed the Scout Green signalbox. Johnny yelled out that their speed had fallen below 20 mph; however, they were now close to the summit of Shap. *Five more shovelfuls and we're over!* thought Johnny and he relaxed for a fraction of a second as he hurled a heavy shovelful of coal down towards the front of the fire. As the coal left the shovel, his hand slid off the handle and the shovel followed its load straight into the Claughton's big firebox, giving his palm a heavy bruise on the way.

Willy stared at his empty hands in shock. From Shap to Carlisle was downhill all the way, but it was also a long 30-mile slope and there were a few level stretches where more shovelling would be needed.

"Johnny!" called Willy, "I've lost my bloody shovel in the firebox!"

"You've done what?" Johnny couldn't believe his ears, "How the hell did you do that?"

"It's my hands; they got all sweaty and with the heavy shovelling, the handle slipped as I threw a load into the box," Willy admitted miserably, rubbing the bruise.

Johnny paused thoughtfully, "We'll have to stop in Penrith and get another shovel; we can't make it to Carlisle otherwise."

"God, I'm so sorry Johnny! And we're 40 minutes down already."

"Can't be helped, Willy, we'll just have to hope they can help us in Penrith; it shouldn't take more than a few minutes and we may be able to catch up at least some of the lost time down through Plumpton and Wreay."

The signals were clear for them through Penrith, but Johnny brought the train to a stop and called a platform porter to get them a new shovel as quickly as possible. This, it turned out, was not as easy as it sounded. The porter returned with the news that the station pilot shunting in the yard was the only engine about and there was no spare shovel in the small engine shed.

"Well, call Plumpton; we can probably manage to get there with the fire as it is. Let them know we need a shovel," said Johnny to the porter. "Right, Willy," the driver said as he eased the train away again, taking great care not to create a strong blast that might lift some of the precious coal off the grate and up the chimney, "let's see if Plumpton can help us."

With Johnny opening the fire doors and Willy throwing large lumps of coal continuously, they managed to reach Plumpton, where a station porter was waiting on the platform for them. He was holding a tiny shovel.

"What in hell am I supposed to do with that?" cried Willy as he saw the shovel.

"It's the on'y shovel we've got," said the porter, grinning at him, "ye'll have to mek do wi' it."

"But it's not a fireman's shovel!"

"Nae, it's the signalman's shovel an' 'e's right angry wi' yer. But 'e ses, 'e'd rather 'ave grubby 'ands from throwin' coal in 'is fire than yer great injin cloggin' 'is tracks all night."

Johnny looked at the shovel as he eased the regulator up to take the train away; he watched as Willy tried to get a heap of coal on the tiny shovel and into the firebox, but said nothing. He turned away to stare out of the window, but Willy saw his shoulders shaking with silent amusement.

The buggers at Crewe North shed will never let me forget this, agonised Willy as he plied the tiny shovel ceaselessly all the way to Carlisle, *and what they'll say when I hand over at Carlisle shed doesn't bear thinking about!*

Some days later, Johnny and Willy took a George V 4-4-0 locomotive light engine from Crewe to Holyhead; it was needed for an ambulance train to collect injured servicemen arriving by ferry from Ireland after the Easter Rising in Dublin. The ambulance train had been marshalled ready for its locomotive to be turned on the turntable and coupled up, and was waiting at the platform for Johnny to back onto the train.

A platform inspector walked up to the cab and called out, "You'll stop at Llandudno Junction, Driver. A naval sloop put in at Llandudno with more wounded, so you'll be picking up another two coaches there."

Johnny waved his acknowledgement as the signal gave him the 'right away', and he eased the ambulance train gently out of the station and up the grade.

"This train may have corridor coaches, Willy, but it's no ordinary passenger train," said Johnny, "we have to give the poor buggers and their nurses an easy ride if we can." They had both seen – and felt for - the wounded soldiers, some still being brought off the Irish ferry, as they backed their George V onto the train.

All the major railway companies were building ambulance trains and by the end of the war about 30 had been constructed. Each coach had a large red cross painted on the side because many of them were built for use in the European theatre of war and might be targeted otherwise.

"Our train even has an operating theatre," commented Johnny, "most of them don't have one of those."

"Not sure I'd want to be operated on if the train was moving," replied Willy. "What if the scalpel slipped?"

"That's why we have to be careful," said Johnny.

Both crewmen took care that the run along the North Welsh coast was as smooth as they could make it and they pulled slowly into Llandudno Junction where they were to stop for the additional coaches. These two were ordinary coaches for sitting wounded, and had been brought in by a small 2-4-2 tank engine, while a shunter climbed down from the platform to the track to couple them to the rear of the ambulance train. He was an Irishmen and called out angrily to the few passengers watching on the platform; "These coaches are full o' murderous Black and Tans; an' if it were up ter me, begorrah, Oi'd drown the boogers in the bloody harbour and send 'em inter hell so that Himself'd see to 'em. Oi'd not give 'em bloody cups er tea an' a sit down in a nice train!"

He jumped down to the track, still muttering imprecations, and lifted the heavy coupling hook as his mate eased the tank engine and its two coaches forward, to push them into position behind the rear coaches of the ambulance train. He was still cursing and swearing as he tried to hold the link ready to drop it over the approaching hook of the rear coach, but he wasn't concentrating and his grip on it loosened; its weight swung him round and he reached out to grab a buffer shank and retain his balance but missed his aim. His hand caught the face of the buffer instead of the shank, just as the two buffers met and crushed his forearm between them. His roar of agony warned the engine driver, who rapidly reversed and drew the two coaches back about a yard, releasing the injured man, who now lay on the ground beneath the coach, clutching his arm and screaming in pain.

Two waiting passengers on the platform jumped down to try and help the shunter, but a doctor called from the ambulance train took one look and jumped into the train then out again a few moments later, carrying a small bag. He dropped onto the track and administered an injection which immediately calmed the shunter's cries. Two orderlies from the train brought down a stretcher and the man was lifted into one of the coaches.

There was a brief consultation between a surgeon and the platform inspector, then the inspector then walked to the front of the train.

"Sorry, Driver," he called to Johnny, "you'll be held up for a half-hour; a shunter has been badly hurt and they're going to amputate his arm because they can't save it. Apparently an amputation doesn't take long, then you can move off while they stabilise him. He'll be disembarked in Chester, where the General Infirmary can look after him. It's due to take half of the wounded troops, anyway; the Great Western will take the rest up to a hospital in Shrewsbury and you can then move light engine back to Crewe North and sign off."

"There you go, Willy," commented Johnny, "they don't operate on the move: next time you lose your shovel and bruise your hand, we can stop the train while they fix you up – and even amputate your mitt, then you won't need to worry about the scalpel slipping!"

20 - The Persistent Malcontent (August 1921)

Jake Henford was a reasonably competent fireman but he had two complaints about his job: he had an intense dislike of being grubby, and he was not fond of heavy work. These were serious hindrances in the life of a footplateman. Steam locomotives were not the cleanest of machines, especially when they were badly in need of maintenance, as most locomotives were after the long years of war. Many of the engines ought to have been sent to the scrapyards long ago, but wartime requirements had kept them in operation long after their use-by date. A further consideration was that the LNWR itself was in financial trouble and was about to be bought by its smaller rival Lancashire and Yorkshire Railway; and who knew then who would keep his job?

It was therefore all the more surprising that he found himself employed as an LNWR fireman, a job in which heavy and dirty physical labour was guaranteed. However, he appreciated one great advantage of his job: as a trained fireman he had been in a reserved occupation and had not been conscripted to fight in the Great War. In 1908, he had been recommended by a distant relative who knew someone at Euston, and as there had been an unexpected vacancy in Camden locomotive shed, Jake had been extremely fortunate in his timing and appointed as a cleaner. In his first years, he had been grateful to have any kind of work and had –unusually - applied himself such that by 1914 he had been promoted to fireman.

One morning, he climbed down from the cab of the Experiment class 4-6-0, exhausted after a difficult run up from Birmingham to Euston. The engine had shown some of the idiosyncrasies that these big express passenger engines were known for on occasions. The steaming had not been easy, in spite of his feverish efforts. His driver, Warren Tranter, had even relieved him a couple of times. While Jake climbed down to uncouple the locomotive from its coaches in order that the station pilot could draw them back to the carriage sidings, he had an idea.

The LNWR had opened its London electric service in 1914, using units with Metro-Cammell coach bodies and Siemens electric motors, and these had proved quite successful. They were planning to extend the limited system but the Great War had intervened and extension of the network was slow. However, by 1921 the network was open as far as Watford.

Jake walked across the platform to a Watford motorman just coming out his cab and put his hand out. "Fireman Jake Henford," he said. "Could you spare me a minute?"

"Yes, of course. My name's Alan Smethwick, by the way."

"I'm thinking of changing over jobs, Mr Smethwick," Jake said, "what's the procedure for becoming a motorman?"

"You want to be a motorman? Why? You've obviously got a steady job as a steam fireman."

"Yes, but a motorman's job is far easier; sitting in a nice warm cab all day, coming off work with a clean collar, you're turning a small handle, not shovelling three tons of coal every shift. You don't even have to climb round the bloody engine, cleaning the motion from the inside. You blokes have it easy!"

"Yeah, well you might have a point; but there's one danger you might have forgotten."

"A danger?"

"Indeed; imagine you're belting through Stafford, you've slowed down to about 50; you're on the regulator and you're looking at a group of passengers on the platform as you flash past."

"Right. So?"

"You don't notice one passenger as he steps off the platform directly in front of you. Then you wonder why your train is stopped at Crewe and the inspectors find part of a human head jammed on your front coupling hook."

"Oh yes, I know that happens sometimes; it's hard to deal with."

"With a motorman, it's quite different. He sees it right under his nose. He's slowing down to stop at Carpenders Park and a passenger jumps off the platform three yards in front of his cab. He's in charge of a 120-ton train travelling at 30; he knows he's about to kill someone and there's bugger-all he can do about it. Many motormen can't handle that; the LNWR loses a few motormen that way; they can't continue in the job, through no fault of their own."

"Yeah, I didn't think of that – but surely that's very rare?"

"Nothing like as rare as you might think – it just doesn't get publicised when it happens."

"Has it ever happened to you?"

"No, and I hope to God it never does. Now, what do you know about electricity?"

"Not much; why?"

"Mainly because you'll be driving electric trains," the motorman spoke with a clearly detectable note of sarcasm.

"Don't you just switch on and off you go?"

The motorman laughed in delight; "I really don't think you're cut out to become a motorman. My advice is for you to just stick to your steamers!"

Jake looked at the motorman again. "I thought your switches do all the electric stuff?"

"You've still got to learn what to do if your train breaks down."

"Don't the fitters do that for you?"

The motorman laughed; "Not when you're half-way to Watford and it's pissing with rain! You have to do that yourself!"

"What about your passengers?"

"What about 'em?"

"Well, what do they do while you're buggering about with the electrics?"

The motorman stared him scornfully. "You're a steam engineman; what do your passengers do if your driver has to fail your engine somewhere on the road?"

"There's nothing they can do, of course."

The motorman nodded. "Exactly," he said and strode off. Then he stopped and turned back. "How did you get to be a qualified fireman?" he called out and walked on without waiting for a reply.

"Cheeky sod!" muttered Jake to himself.

It was very hot in the cab of their tank engine and they were parked near the carriage sidings at Watford, where some electric trains were stabled. Jake looked at them with interest. He could see that one of the motormen's cab doors was open and he stared inside. It didn't seem to be overly complex, and he could see himself sitting in comfort while gliding along at a gentle 35 miles per hour, merely holding on to the handle and watching for the signals. It really didn't look as complex as Motorman Smethwick had implied. He decided to have a closer look and, as they had a half-hour break, climbed down to walk to the motorman's cab and smoke a cigarette. A piece of wood had broken off and was lying across a nearby rail. Jake sat down on it.

A motorman appeared after a few minutes, strolling towards him, but stopped dead and stared as he caught sight of Jake smoking. His face paled. "Wh-what the hell are you doing?" he stuttered.

"I'm having a smoke, of course," said Jake in surprise, "what's wrong with that?"

The motorman shook his head, "Look, mate, get off that piece of wood very carefully, and for god's sake don't touch the rail with your bare hands!"

"What? Why?"

"Because you're sitting on a live rail, you bloody fool, and I'm sure you don't want 630 volts up your arse!"

"Christ!" muttered Jake and rose carefully off the rail. "I saw the piece of wood and thought it would make a handy seat!" he said shakily.

"It would've made a handy electric chair!" said the motorman grimly. "You're very lucky to be alive. I'd stay clear of the electrics if I were you."

One very cold November evening, they were approaching London on an up Euston express. As they slowed down at the signal gantry just before Camden, Jake noticed an electric train stopped with a man - presumably its motorman - with what looked like some kind of wooden spade in his hand, hitting the live rail in front of his train.

"Hey Mr Tranter, come and have a butcher's at this," Jake called to his driver.

"What?"

"That poor bloody motorman out on the track. What the hell's he doing?"

"Oh that, he's cleaning the ice off the live rail. My cousin's a motorman and he curses the very cold weather."

"Why?"

"When the ice freezes on the live rail, the shoes can't pick up the current, and the only thing you can do is to get out and try and remove it."

"Poor buggers!"

"Yes," added his driver, "we don't have that problem; our energy comes from the coal in this here tender - and your muscles put it into our fire," he added, grinning.

"What if he can't shift the ice?"

"He can't move his train and has to go to fetch help. It's a common problem with the electrics in winter."

"Can't he send his guard?"

"The bloke's on his own in the cab, and the guard's in charge anyway, like he is with us. We can't give orders to our guard, either."

"Hmm, yes," admitted Jake, "I hadn't thought of that."

Over the next few weeks, Jake thought long and hard about

applying to become a motorman, as he still considered that life was considerably easier in the cab of an electric train. He borrowed a book from the local library on electricity and it really didn't seem overly complex. He was sure he could pick up what else was needed in a couple of days in the cab of an electric with the instructor watching at his side. And yes, well, he might have to put up with an occasional nip outside to pat the ice on the rail or take off the shoe or whatever it was you had to do, but he could live with that. It would certainly beat the need to shovel five tons of coal into the firebox of an Experiment with attitude on a boat train to Liverpool.

Some months later, Jake was in a classroom with several other enginemen, listening to a senior motorman explaining the intricacies of the power arrangements of the LNWR's electric trains. Jake had no intention of staying in a steam cab for the rest of his working life. He had elected, therefore, to request a transfer to motorman duties, believing that he would, by dint of careful study, finally be able to get the hang of the job. However, fate seemed determined to set hurdles in his way. The instructor in his training class was very thorough; firstly, they had been told to forget everything they knew about steam locomotives; an electric unit was a totally different kettle of fish. There were air pumps, collector shoes, condensers, relays and other complicated-sounding terms to become familiar with, and very little time in which to do this. Furthermore, all they seemed to be learning was what to do if things went wrong. In fact, Jake's only previous correct impression concerned the time taken to start and finish a shift. In a steam locomotive, 45 minutes to an hour was needed for engine preparation, and another half-hour or so was required at the end of the shift to check that the engine was in a condition ready for the next driver to take over. In an electric unit, the respective times were ten minutes at the beginning and five to switch off at the end. Aside from that and his understanding of the signals, there was almost nothing else in common with firing or driving a steam locomotive.

The sessions in the classroom were increasingly frustrating; every day there were more complications to memorise, with the appropriate vocabulary, and the class were all hauled out one freezing morning to clear ice from a section of a live rail.

"You're lucky to be able to have this experience, lads," commented the instructor. "It's rare that you learn to do this under supervision. Mostly, motormen have to learn on the job, but since we're in the middle of winter, you get to do it with me watching."

Jake did not feel at all lucky; his yard of iced rail was particularly obstinate, and he was in a foul mood. Yesterday's session in the cab of an electric unit had been totally confusing, and finally he had lost his temper and attempted to kick the rail. His leg did not move; it was held tight by the arm of the instructor, who had been watching him carefully.

"You can electrocute yourself later if you want to, Fireman Henford, but you're not doing it on my watch. Now, collect your things and leave my class. You don't have the attitude to be a safe motorman; if I hadn't grabbed your leg, you'd be dead by now. Go back to your steam locomotives and be thankful you're still alive."

A badly shaking Jake stammered a brief words of thanks and walked away. Finally, he conceded that the electrics were clearly not for him.

The Engines

Precedent (Jumbos): first constructed 1874. These 2-4-0 passenger engines were nicknamed 'Jumbos' because of their prodigious feats for their small size. Relegated to lesser duties by 1900.

Jubilee: first constructed 1897. Intended to be big engines to replace the over-worked Precedents, these 4-4-0s were sluggish and not a success.

Precursor: first constructed 1904. At last, a highly successful, straightforward 4-4-0 for express passenger duties.

Experiment: first constructed 1905. Designed to take express trains more easily over hilly runs, these 4-6-0s were based on the Precursor but were slower and difficult to fire.

Prince of Wales: first constructed 1911. Improved and redesigned versions of the Experiments, these express engines were excellent workhorses from the outset.

Claughton: first constructed 1913. Large, powerful 4-6-0 express engines, the onset of the First World War thwarted effort to overcome 'bugs' that hindered their great potential.

Ramsbottom (Special) tank: first constructed 1870. Of ancient ancestry and appearance, these celebrated but cab-less 0-6-0T tanks afforded little crew protection during their short-run and shunting duties. Short roofs were added later.

Coal tank: first constructed 1881. These simple, cheap 0-6-2T tank engines were designed for coal and goods traffic, but sometimes undertook passenger duties on country lines.

Watford tank: first constructed 1898. Based on express goods engines, these competent 0-6-2T tanks had larger wheels suited to local passenger services, especially around London.

Technical vocabulary

Banking engine: An engine at the rear of a train assisting by pushing from behind.

Bobby: railway signalmen. The name derives from Sir Robert Peel's police force.

Brake van: small van at the end of a goods train from which the guard could apply a brake to assist the driver when slowing the train. In a passenger train, the brake van would be a coach with a section for the guard.

Brighton Line: Railwaymen's term for the London, Brighton & South Coast Railway.

Caley: railway slang for the Caledonian Railway.

Distant: a signal warning drivers about the status of the section following the one they were entering. (see also 'home' and 'starter')

Driver: the man who controls the locomotive.

Down: the direction from London. (see also **'Up'**)

Fireman: the man who ensures that the locomotive has sufficient energy for the driver to do his job. Earlier commentaries refer to the fireman as a 'stoker'.

Guard: the official in charge of a train; he was normally at the rear of the train.

Home: a signal indicating whether the next section is clear. (see also **'distant'** and **'starter'**)

Horsebox: a van specially fitted out for transporting horses.

Lanky: slang name for the Lancashire and Yorkshire Railway

Light engine: an engine travelling without a train.

Link: a group of drivers in a shed who were allotted to similar duties. The 'top link' drivers were those with the highest priority trains.

Motion: the set of coupling and connecting rods linking the driving wheels and the cylinders.

Pilot engine: engine which would be coupled in front of a train engine and used to assist with a heavy train.

Salop: railway term for Shrewsbury, based on the original Latin.

Semi-fast: a train which does not stop at all stations.

Starter: a signal (usually at the end of a platform) to indicate whether a train may move off to the next signal. (see also **'home'** and **'distant'**)

Stoker: see 'fireman'.

Stopper: a train which calls at all stations on its run.

Turntable: a large, revolving table in an engine shed. It permits engines to be turned round.

Up: the direction to London.

If you have enjoyed this book, we would be very grateful if you would take the time to review it on the Amazon website. A positive review is invaluable. It can help new readers decide whether they would like to buy a book, and will be greatly appreciated by the author.

Please also visit the Heddon Publishing website to find out about our other titles: **www.heddonpublishing.com**

Heddon Publishing was established in 2012 and is a publishing house with a difference. We work with independent authors to get their work out into the real world, by-passing the traditional slog through 'slush piles'.
Please contact us by email in the first instance to find out more: enquiries@heddonpublishing.com

Like us on Facebook and receive all our news at:
www.facebook.com/heddonpublishing

Join our mailing list by emailing:
mailinglist@heddonpublishing.com

Follow us on Twitter: @PublishHeddon

Printed in Great Britain
by Amazon